Close Reading with Paired Texts

Level 5

Engaging Lessons
to Improve
Comprehension

Authors
Lori Oczkus, M.A.
Timothy Rasinski, Ph.D.

Digital Texts

To obtain digital copies of all the texts in this resource, scan the QR code or visit our website at **http://www.shelleducation.com/paired-texts/**.

Publishing Credits

Corinne Burton, M.A.Ed., *President*; Jodene Lynn Smith, M.A., *Contributing Author*; Emily R. Smith, M.A.Ed., *Content Director*; Jennifer Wilson, *Editor*; Courtney Patterson, *Multimedia Designer*; Monique Dominguez, *Production Artist*; Stephanie Bernard, *Assistant Editor*; Amber Goff, *Editorial Assistant*

Image Credits

Library of Congress: p. 12, p. 93; iStock: p. 7, p. 15; NOAA: p. 102; All other images Shutterstock

Standards

© 2004 Mid-continent Research for Education and Learning (McREL)

© 2007 Teachers of English to Speakers of Other Languages, Inc. (TESOL)

© 2007 Board of Regents of the University of Wisconsin System. World-Class Instructional Design and Assessment (WIDA)

© Copyright 2010. National Governors Association Center for Best Practices and Council of Chief State School Officers. All rights reserved. (CCSS)

Shell Education

5301 Oceanus Drive
Huntington Beach, CA 92649-1030
http://www.shelleducation.com

ISBN 978-1-4258-1361-1

© 2015 Shell Educational Publishing, Inc.

Table of Contents

About Close Reading

What Is Close Reading?

Students today need to carry a "tool kit" of effective reading strategies to help them comprehend a wide variety of texts. Close reading is one way for students to enhance their understanding especially as they read more challenging texts. The Common Core State Standards (2010) call for students to "read closely to determine what the text says explicitly and to make logical inferences from it and cite specific textual evidence when writing or speaking to support conclusions drawn from the text." Instead of skipping or glossing over difficult texts, students need to develop strategies for digging into the text on their own (Fisher and Frey 2012). Good readers dig deeper as they read and reread a text for a variety of important purposes. Close reading involves rereading to highlight, underline, reconsider points, ask and answer questions, consider author's purpose and word choice, develop appropriate oral expression and fluency, and discuss the text with others. In close reading lessons, students learn to exercise the discipline and concentration for analyzing the text at hand rather than heading off topic. Students of all ages can be taught to carefully reread challenging texts on their own for a variety of purposes.

> Close reading involves rereading to highlight, underline, reconsider points, ask and answer questions, consider author's purpose and word choice, develop appropriate oral expression and fluency, and discuss the text with others.

Reciprocal Teaching, or the "Fab Four," and Close Reading

Reciprocal teaching is a scaffolded discussion technique that involves four of the most critical comprehension strategies that good readers employ to comprehend text—**predict**, **clarify**, **question**, and **summarize** (Oczkus 2010; Palincsar and Brown 1986). We refer to the reciprocal teaching strategies as "The Fab Four" (Oczkus 2012). These strategies may be discussed in any order but must all be included in every lesson. Together the four strategies form a powerful package that strengthens comprehension. Research has found that students who engage in reciprocal teaching show improvement in as little as 15 days (Palincsar and Brown 1986) by participating more eagerly in discussions. After just three to six months they may grow one to two years in their reading levels (Rosenshine and Meister 1994; Hattie 2008).

The reciprocal teaching strategies make it a practical lesson pattern for close readings. First, students briefly glance over a text to anticipate and predict the author's purpose, topic or theme, and text organization. As students read, they make note of words or phrases they want to clarify. During questioning, students reread to ask and answer questions and provide evidence from the text. Finally, students reread again to summarize and respond to the text. Quick partner and team cooperative discussions throughout the process increase students' comprehension and critical thinking. A strong teacher think-aloud component also pushes student thinking and provides students the modeling and support they need to learn to read challenging texts on their own. The four strategies become the tool kit students rely on as they read any text closely.

About Close Reading (cont)

What Is Reading Fluency?

Fluency refers to the ability to read and understand the words encountered in texts accurately and automatically or effortlessly (Rasinski 2010). All readers come to a text with a limited or finite amount of cognitive resources. If they have to use too much of their cognitive resources to decode the words in the text, they have less of these resources available for the more important task in reading—comprehension. Readers who are not automatic in word recognition are easy to spot. They read text slowly and laboriously, often stopping at difficult words to figure them out. Although they may be able to accurately read the words, their comprehension suffers because too much of their attention had to be devoted to word recognition and away from comprehension. So although accuracy in word recognition is good, it is not enough. Fluency also includes automaticity. Good readers are fluent readers.

Fluency also has another component. It is prosody, or expressive reading. Fluent readers read orally with expression and phrasing that reflect and enhance the meaning of the passage (Rasinski 2010). Research has demonstrated that readers who are accurate, automatic, and expressive in their oral reading tend to be readers who read orally *and* silently with good comprehension. Moreover, students who perform poorly on tests of silent reading comprehension exhibit difficulties in one or more areas of reading fluency.

Fluency and Close Reading

How does a person become fluent? The simple answer is practice. However, there are various forms of practice in reading that nurture fluency in students. Students need to hear and talk about fluent reading from and with more proficient readers. In doing so, they develop an understanding of what actually constitutes fluent reading.

Fluency should be an essential part of close reading. Without some degree of fluency, it is difficult for students to successfully engage in close reading. If readers have to invest too much cognitive energy into the lower-level tasks of word recognition, they will have less energy available for the tasks required of close reading— interpreting author's purpose, noting detailed information, making inferences, etc. Close reading, by definition, requires readers to read a text more than once for different purposes. Reading a text more than once is called *repeated reading*. Moreover, one of the purposes for repeated reading can and should be to read a passage with a level of fluency that reflects the meaning of the text (Rasinski and Griffith 2010). For fluency strategies to use with students, see page 124.

By combining close reading using reciprocal teaching strategies with fluency, we end up with greater reading benefits for students than if close reading and fluency were taught and practiced separately. It is simply more efficient, more effective, and more authentic to deal with both of these critical competencies together. We call it *synergy*. Your students will call it *fun*!

About Close Reading (cont)

Why Pair Fiction and Nonfiction Texts?

Standards point out that from the initial stages of literacy development, students need exposure to both fiction and nonfiction texts. Yet the previous conventional wisdom was to focus primarily on fiction and gradually move toward more nonfiction. We provide a balance of the two texts throughout this book. In doing so, we give students opportunities to explore and gain proficiency in close reading strategies with a range of text types.

When pairing texts, we also provide a content connection between them. One passage can help build background knowledge, while the other passage focuses on building interest. Our paired texts allow students to engage in comparing and contrasting various types of texts, which in itself is a form of close reading.

The pairing of texts also helps students see that different forms of texts may require different levels or types of reading fluency. Fiction, including poetry, is written with voice. Authors and poets try to embed a voice in their writing that they wish the reader to hear. Texts written with voice should be read with expression. Thus, these texts lend themselves extremely well to reading with appropriate fluency. While nonfiction may also be written with voice, it is a different type of writing that often requires a different form of expression and fluency. By pairing these forms of texts, we offer students opportunities to master fluent reading in two forms.

Since multiple reading encounters with the same text are required in close reading activities, you will notice the texts are not very long. Students will be able to reread the engaging texts for multiple purposes to achieve greater success with their comprehension of the texts.

Close Reading and Differentiation

The close reading lessons in this resource are filled with many options for scaffolding to meet the needs of all students, including English language learners and struggling readers. The lessons offer a variety of stopping points where the teacher can choose to think aloud and provide specific modeling, coaching, and feedback. Understanding your students' background knowledge and interests will help you decide whether you should read the informational texts first or grab students' interests by starting with the fictional texts. Throughout the lessons, vocabulary is addressed in a variety of creative ways that will help students who struggle to better understand the text. Sentence frames, such as *I think I will learn _____ because_____* or *I didn't get the word _____, so I _____*, provide students with a focus for their rereading tasks and discussions with peers. Creative options for rereading the texts to build fluency and comprehension give students who need more support lots of meaningful practice.

Effective Tips for Close Reading Lessons

To make the most out of close reading lessons, be sure to include the following:

1. **Text Focus**

   Throughout the lessons, keep the main focus on the text itself by examining how it is organized, the author's purpose, text evidence, and reasons why the author chose certain words or visuals.

2. **Think Alouds**

   Model close reading using teacher think alouds to help make thinking visible to students. For example, before asking students to find words to clarify, demonstrate by choosing a word from the text and showing different ways to clarify it.

3. **Cooperative Learning**

   Students' comprehension increases when they discuss the reading with others. Ask partners or groups to "turn and talk" during every step of the lesson.

4. **Scaffolding**

   Some students need extra support with comprehension or fluency. Use the suggestions on pages 123–124 that include sentence frames, ways to reread the text, props, gestures, and other ideas to reach every learner and make the lessons engaging.

5. **Metacognition/Independence**

   Name the rereading steps for students throughout the lessons. This will help them remember how to read closely when they encounter rigorous texts on their own. For example, before questioning say, "Now let's reread the text to find evidence as we ask and answer our questions."

Adapted from Lori D. Oczkus (2010)

A Close Reading Snapshot

Below is an example showing what one lesson might look like.

Mrs. Chen passes out the informational text about storms. Students participate in a quick and quiet text walk to anticipate the author's purpose and the topic. As students read the text silently, they circle words that are related to weather. Mrs. Chen reads aloud once through, modeling fluency. The students reread the text in small teams as they underline challenging words and ideas that they want to clarify. Using evidence from the text, students compare and contrast convection air in hurricanes and tornadoes. Then, students work in groups to create props and costumes as they prepare to perform the text.

Lesson Plan Overview

Teacher Pages

The lessons have overview pages that include summaries of the themes students will focus on and and answer keys. Each lesson include two Teacher Notes charts, one for the nonfiction text and one for the fiction text. Both charts follow the same structure as below. **Note:** You will find some teacher modeling suggestions in the right hand columns of the charts. Prior to implementing the lessons, provide students with copies of the texts to mark throughout the lessons, and project larger versions of the texts for the class to see so that you can model important steps in the close-reading process. You can find digital copies of the texts at **http://www.shelleducation.com/paired-texts/**.

Lesson Steps	Purpose
Ready, Set, Predict!	In this section, students will: • skim the text • anticipate the topic • think about the author's purpose • think about text organization
Go!	In this section, students will: • read the text independently • anticipate the topic • think about the author's purpose • think about text organization • listen to the teacher read the text aloud • reread the text for various purposes • focus on various aspects of fluency
Reread to Clarify	In this section, students will: • work independently, in pairs, or in small groups to reread the text and identify words or phrases they want to clarify • use various clarifying strategies such as sounding out, studying word parts, visualizing content, and rereading
Reread to Question	In this section, students will: • work independently, in pairs, or in small groups to reread the text and ask and answer questions about the text • use text evidence to answer questions that are self-generated or asked by the teacher
Reread to Summarize and Respond	In this section, students will: • work independently, in pairs, or in small groups to reread the text and summarize the main ideas and details • evaluate the text • share text evidence to support their summaries of the text

Lesson Plan Overview (cont.)

Student Pages

After reading each pair of fiction and nonfiction texts, the lesson plan continues with opportunities for comparing the two texts and creative follow-up options that can be conducted with the whole class, small groups, partners, or as independent work in a center.

Response Pages

Each text has a follow-up activity page where students use their knowledge of the text to answer text-dependent questions.

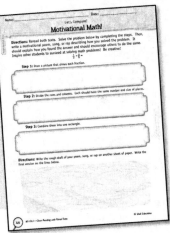

Comparing the Texts

This activity page offers creative reasons for students to reread both texts and synthesize information from both to accomplish a task. A few examples include: writing a news account, writing a poem, filling in a graphic organizer, or making a game.

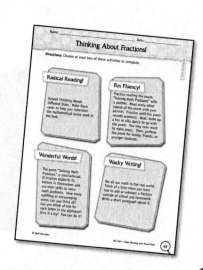

All About the Content

This activity page offers four activities that students can choose from that focus on their comprehension of the paired texts. The activities have the same focus in each lesson: reading, fluency, word study, and writing.

Theme Summary

Prejudice is an important word for students to understand. Students need to embrace tolerance and learn to respect those who are different from themselves. In this pair of texts, students will read and respond to a poem by Paul Laurence Dunbar and a speech by Robert Kennedy announcing the death of Dr. Martin Luther King Jr. This text pair will enrich and enlighten students' impressionable minds.

Answer Key

"A Difficult Day" Response (page 13)

1. D. an effort to understand

2. Do Need: love, wisdom, and compassion toward one another
   Do Not Need: division, hatred, violence, or lawlessness

3. The three things that the vast majority of people in America want to live together, to improve the quality of life, and to have justice for all humans.

"Sympathy" Response (page 16)

1. C. a prayer

2. The bird wants to *be free* and would rather be on a *bough a-swing* then in a cage.

3. The author sympathizes with the bird and shares the same desires of freedom. That's why he uses the phrase *I know* throughout the poem. He knows how the bird feels.

Let's Compare! Pledge Against Prejudice (page 17)

Students' pledges will vary, but should include words from the provided word bank.

Standards

➡ Determine a theme of a story, drama, or poem from details in the text, including how characters in a story or drama respond to challenges or how the speaker in a poem reflects upon a topic.

➡ Explain the relationships or interactions between two or more individuals, events, ideas, or concepts in a historical, scientific, or technical text based on specific information in the text.

➡ Demonstrate understanding of figurative language, word relationships, and nuances in word meanings.

Materials

➡ *A Difficult Day* (pages 12–13)

➡ *"A Difficult Day" Response* (page 13)

➡ *Sympathy* (page 15)

➡ *"Sympathy" Response* (page 16)

➡ *Let's Compare! Pledge Against Prejudice* (page 17)

➡ *Thinking About Prejudice!* (page 18)

➡ pencils

➡ online resources

Comparing the Texts

After students complete the lessons for each text, have them work in pairs or groups to reread both texts and complete the *Let's Compare! Pledge Against Prejudice* activity page (page 17). Finally, students can work to complete the *Thinking About Prejudice!* matrix (page 18). The matrix activities allow students to work on the important literacy skills of reading, writing, vocabulary, and fluency.

Nonfiction Text Teacher Notes
A Difficult Day

	Lesson Steps	Teacher Think Alouds
Ready, Set, Predict!	• Read the title aloud. Tell students this text is about Dr. Martin Luther King Jr. and Senator Robert Kennedy (President John F. Kennedy's younger brother). Ask students to use prior knowledge to list what they already know about these men. **Note:** You may wish to have students research information about Robert Kennedy prior to implementing the activity. • Have partners share their lists.	"Before I begin to read a text, I stop and think of all the things I already know about the topic. This helps me to better understand what I am about to read."
Go!	• Provide the text to students and display a larger version of it. Ask students to read the text independently. When students are finished, read the text aloud. Model fluent reading and pausing. • Pair students. Have them reread the text one more time together. Challenge students to circle any words they think younger students might find tricky.	
 **Reread to Clarify**	• Tell students to reread the text to clarify it. Discuss the different strategies students can use to clarify the words they circled in the *Go!* section (e.g., *discuss with a partner, reread, read on*). • Have students discuss the words they circle and the strategies they use to clarify them.	"I do not know what the word *lawlessness* means, so I chop it into parts. I know what the word *law* means. I know the suffix *-less* means 'without' and *-ness* means the 'state of,' therefore the word means 'having no laws.'"
 **Reread to Question**	• Ask students to reread the text to question. Instruct partners to select and reread paragraphs. Then, ask them to form discussion questions to ask other pairs about their paragraphs. • Direct students to use evidence from the text while discussing prejudice and tolerance. • Have students respond to the question and prompts on page 13.	"As I read the second paragraph, I want to ask the question 'Why does the senator not give the speech he originally planned on giving?' By asking this question, I am able to remember that Mr. Luther King Jr. was killed, and the senator wanted to share the sad news with the crowd."
Reread to Summarize and Respond	• Tell students to reread the text to summarize. Have them share aloud anything new they learned about prejudice, tolerance, Dr. King, or Senator Kennedy. • Invite students to add these items to the lists they made at the beginning of the lesson.	

*Note: For more tips, engagement strategies, and fluency options to include in this lesson, see pages 122–128.

Language Arts Texts

A Difficult Day

April 4, 1968, was a sad day for Americans. Martin Luther King Jr. was shot and killed. Dr. King had spent most of his life fighting for equal rights for African Americans. He wanted all people to be treated the same under the law.

One very sad person that day was Robert F. Kennedy. He was the younger brother of former President John F. Kennedy. At the time, he was a United States senator from New York. The senator was in Indianapolis, Indiana, to give a speech to a group of African Americans. Kennedy had just heard the news about Dr. King's death. He realized the crowd did not know yet. He did not give the speech he had planned. Instead, he told the sad news to the crowd. Here are some excerpts from what he said.

"I have some very sad news for all of you, and, I think, sad news for all of our fellow citizens, and people who love peace all over the world, and that is that Martin Luther King was shot and was killed tonight in Memphis, Tennessee."

"Martin Luther King dedicated his life to love and to justice between fellow human beings. He died in the cause of that effort. In this difficult day, in this difficult time for the United States, it's perhaps well to ask what kind of a nation we are and what direction we want to move in. . . . you can be filled with bitterness, and with hatred, and a desire for revenge."

"Or we can make an effort, as Martin Luther King did, to understand, and to comprehend, and replace that violence, that stain of bloodshed that has spread across our land, with an effort to understand, compassion and love."

"For those of you who are black and are tempted to be filled with hatred and mistrust of the injustice of such an act, against all white people, I would only say that I can also feel in my own heart the same kind of feeling. I had a member of my family killed, but he was killed by a white man. But we have to make an effort in the United States, we have to make an effort to understand, to get beyond or go beyond these rather difficult times."

"What we need in the United States is not division. What we need in the United States is not hatred; what we need in the United States is not violence and lawlessness; but is love and wisdom, and compassion toward one another . . ."

A Difficult Day *(cont)*

"We can do well in this country. We will have difficult times; we've had difficult times in the past; and we will have difficult times in the future. It is not the end of violence; it is not the end of lawlessness; and it is not the end of disorder."

"But the vast majority of white people and the vast majority of black people in this country want to live together, want to improve the quality of our life, and want justice for all human beings that abide in our land."

- -

"A Difficult Day" Response

Directions: Reread the text on pages 12–13 to answer each question.

1. What should Americans replace violence with according to Senator Kennedy?

   Ⓐ freedom and justice   Ⓒ revenge

   Ⓑ bloodshed   Ⓓ an effort to understand

2. Use the text to make a list of what Senator Kennedy says Americans need and what they do not need.

   Do Need   **Do Not Need**

   _____   _____

   _____   _____

   _____   _____

3. According to the senator's speech, what are the three things the vast majority of the people in America want?

   _____

   _____

   _____

Fiction Text Teacher Notes
Sympathy

	Lesson Steps	Teacher Think Alouds
Ready, Set, Predict!	• Provide the text to students and display a larger version. Ask them to do an independent text walk to predict the theme of the poem using the title and words they see. • Have partners discuss their ideas using the following: *I think this poem is about _____ because _____.* • Review the type of poem with students.	"This is a lyric poem. That means it conveys deep personal feelings in a way that is similar to a song. Knowing this will help me to better understand the poem."
Go!	• Ask students to read the poem silently to think about the content and to circle words they want to discuss or know more about. • Read the text aloud as students follow along. Discuss the theme of captivity with students. • Tell students to reread the text with partners and underline words and phrases having to do with the theme of captivity.	"I see the phrase *caged bird* throughout the poem. I am going to underline each time it appears to help me remember that the theme of the poem is captivity."
Reread to Clarify	• Have partners reread the poem to clarify by drawing boxes around words or phrases that help them to visualize the theme of captivity. Have partners discuss their boxed words or phrases using the following: *The word/phrase _____ helps me visualize because _____.*	
Reread to Question	• Tell students to reread the text to question. Discuss the use of figurative language in the poem. Guide students to discuss the implied metaphor that compares the caged bird to an oppressed human. Ask each student to choose one metaphor and create a question about it to ask a partner. • Have students respond to the question and prompts on page 16.	
Reread to Summarize and Respond	• Ask partners to reread the text and verbally summarize the poem in their own words. • Invite students to draw illustrations that express their feelings about the poem. Have them share their illustrations with partners.	"Summarizing the text and putting it in my own words helps me to better understand the theme and the word meanings in the poem."

*Note: For more tips, engagement strategies, and fluency options to include in this lesson, see pages 122–128.

Name:_____ Date:_____

Sympathy

by Paul Laurence Dunbar

I know what the caged bird feels, alas!
    When the sun is bright on the upland slopes;
When the wind stirs soft through the springing grass,
And the river flows like a stream of glass;
    When the first bird sings and the first bud opens,
And the faint perfume from its chalice steals—
I know what the caged bird feels!

I know why the caged bird beats his wing
    Till its blood is red on the cruel bars;
For he must fly back to his perch and cling
When he fain would be on the bough a-swing;
    And a pain still throbs in the old, old scars
And they pulse again with a keener sting—
I know why he beats his wing!

I know why the caged bird sings, ah me,
    When his wing is bruised and his bosom sore—
When he beats his bars and he would be free;
It is not a carol of joy or glee,
    But a prayer that he sends from his heart's deep core,
But a plea, that upward to heaven he flings—
I know why the caged bird sings!

"Sympathy" Response

Directions: Reread the poem on page 15 to answer each question.

1. To what does the poet compare the caged bird's song?

   Ⓐ a carol of joy   Ⓒ a prayer

   Ⓑ a carol of glee   Ⓓ a stream

2. What phrases does the poet use to describe what the bird wants?

   _____

   _____

   _____

   _____

   _____

3. Use evidence from the poem to explain why you think the author chose "Sympathy" as the title of the poem.

   _____

   _____

   _____

   _____

   _____

Name:_____ Date:_____

Let's Compare!

Pledge Against Prejudice

Directions: Reread both texts. Use the texts and the words in the Word Bank to help you write your own pledge against prejudice. Your pledge should explain ways in which you will avoid prejudice and promote tolerance. After you write your pledge, practice reading it. Then, share it with your friends and family.

Word Bank					
tolerance	speak up	support	acceptance	open minded	civil rights
stereotypes	racism	prejudice	discrimination	bullying	respect

My Pledge Against Prejudice

I pledge to _____

_____

_____

_____

_____

_____

_____

_____

_____

_____

Thinking About Prejudice!

Directions: Choose at least two of these activities to complete.

Radical Reading

Reread "Sympathy." What are the most powerful lines in the poem? Which lines make the biggest impression on you? Highlight these lines. Then, write a few words explaining why you chose them.

Fun Fluency

Reread "A Difficult Day." Imagine you have to give Senator Kennedy's speech. What tone would you use? Which words would you emphasize? Practice reading and reciting the excerpts from Senator Kennedy's speech. Perform the speech for a classmate.

Wonderful Words

In line four of the poem, "Sympathy," the poet writes *the river flows like a stream of glass*. Write another simile that could replace this line in the poem. Share your simile with a partner.

Wacky Writing

Imagine you are a newspaper reporter covering Senator Robert F. Kennedy's speech that day. Write an article about what happened. Summarize what the senator said. Include how you think the crowd reacts to his speech.

Extreme Weather

Theme Summary

The sky grows dark. The wind picks up. A big storm is approaching. But just how big is it? Extreme weather is frightening. It is also fascinating (from a safe distance, of course). In this unit, students will read and respond to a reader's theater script on tornadoes and a nonfiction text piece about tornadoes and hurricanes. The forecast for this pair of texts is wild and windy fun!

Standards

➡ Quote accurately from a text when explaining what the text says explicitly and when drawing inferences from the text.

➡ Explain the relationships or interactions between two or more individuals, events, ideas, or concepts in a historical, scientific, or technical text based on specific information in the text.

➡ Engage effectively in a range of collaborative discussions with diverse partners on grade 5 topics and texts, building on others' ideas and expressing their own clearly.

Materials

➡ *Severe Storms* (page 21)

➡ *"Severe Storms" Response* (page 22)

➡ *Touchdown of the Wrong Kind* (pages 24–25)

➡ *"Touchdown of the Wrong Kind" Response* (page 25)

➡ *Let's Compare! Weird Weather!* (page 26)

➡ *Thinking About Extreme Weather!* (page 27)

➡ pencils

Comparing the Texts

After students complete the lessons for each text, have them work in pairs or groups to reread both texts and complete the *Let's Compare! Weird Weather!* activity page (page 26). Finally, students can work to complete the *Thinking About Extreme Weather!* matrix (page 27). The matrix activities allow students to work on the important literacy skills of reading, writing, vocabulary, and fluency.

Answer Key

"Severe Storms" Response (page 22)

1. C. warm ocean water

2. The author includes that warm air is spun into a vortex by horizontal winds and that it is a funnel shape made with spinning energy that tilts into a vertical position and spins to gain more energy.

3. The author describes density as *how much matter is in a certain space.*

"Touchdown of the Wrong Kind" Response (page 25)

1. B. a severe thunderstorm

2. Wendy says that condensation is when a *gas turns into a liquid.*

3. A mesocyclone is created when *wind shears cause the updraft and downdraft that move around.*

Let's Compare! Weird Weather! (page 26)

Students' posters will vary. Check that facts and visuals on the posters are correct.

Nonfiction Text Teacher Notes
Severe Storms

Lesson Steps	Teacher Think Alouds
Ready, Set, Predict! • Provide students with the text and display a larger version. Have them skim the text. • Ask partners to predict the author's purpose using the following: *I think the author wrote this text to _____* (e.g., *inform, persuade, entertain*) *because _____.*	"When I read a text, it helps me to think about why the author wrote it. Is the author trying to persuade me to think a certain way about a topic? Is the author trying to make me laugh or cry? Is the author trying to educate me on a particular topic?"
Go! • Tell students to read the text independently to think about the content and to circle words related to weather. • Read the text aloud to students. Model fluent reading. • Ask students to write sentences that include one of the words they circle and explain what they learn from the word.	"Circling specific parts of the text helps me focus my attention on a specific area and gives me a better understanding of the text as a whole."
Reread to Clarify • Tell small groups to reread the text to clarify. Ask group members to underline parts of the text that they find confusing. • Have groups work together to clarify the parts each member underline using the following: *The part where _____ is confusing, so we _____.*	"The part where the author writes about air density is confusing, so we draw illustrations to help us better understand what the text is saying."
Reread to Question • Direct partners to reread the text to question. Have them answer this question using evidence from the text: *How are hurricanes and tornadoes the same and different?* • Open a class discussion on severe storms. Invite students to build on each others' ideas and express their own ideas clearly using evidence from the text. • Have students respond to the question and prompts on page 22.	"When I create questions or answers for a text, I make sure to mark the information I need to remember. This helps me focus my attention on the specific information. To help me remember how they are the same, I will underline the lines *Energy for a hurricane is the result of convection from warm ocean water* and *Convection currents also form tornadoes.*"
Reread to Summarize and Respond • Tell partners to reread the text to summarize. Have them take turns summarizing it by acting out what they think are the three most important points in the text. • Review the close reading strategies by singing the song on page 128.	

*Note: For more tips, engagement strategies, and fluency options to include in this lesson, see pages 122–128.

Name:_____ Date:_____

Severe Storms

by Jack L. Roberts

Have you ever watched the sky during a storm? Storms happen because of convection. Convection is the up-and-down motion of air. It is caused by heat. As air warms, its density decreases. Density describes how much matter is in a certain amount of space. Air that is less dense rises, and it moves from the bottom of the atmosphere to the top. This causes clouds to form. The air in the clouds cools, and the density of the air increases. It moves in a cycle back to the surface. Convection helps keep Earth's temperature livable. Without convection, Earth's temperature would get too hot. But convection also causes extreme weather, such as hurricanes and tornadoes.

Energy for a hurricane is the result of convection from warm ocean water. Oceans are powerful sources of energy. In hurricanes, warm water heats the air above them. The air rises as it warms. This creates an area of low pressure. Higher-pressure air from surrounding areas moves in (as high-speed winds) to take the place of the rising warm air. This gets the storm started. The air is then warmed and rises. This leads to more high-pressure air coming in to replace the rising warm air. The cycle continues, causing a hurricane.

Convection currents also form tornadoes. A tornado happens because a warm, moist air mass meets a cool, dry air mass. The warm air rises over the cooler air. When conditions are right, the warm air is spun into a vortex by horizontal winds higher in the atmosphere. A vortex is a funnel shape made by spinning energy. Rising air tilts the vortex into a vertical, or upright, position. As the vortex spins, it gains energy, forming a tornado.

Hurricanes and tornadoes are extreme examples of both severe storms and powerful energy movement. Both types of storms are very dangerous.

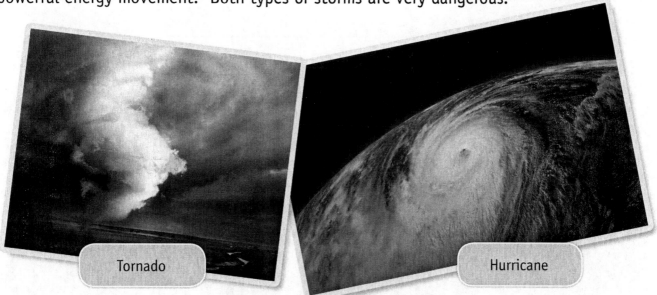

Tornado

Hurricane

Name:_____ Date: _____

"Severe Storms" Response

Directions: Reread the text on page 21 to answer each question.

1. Where does a hurricane get its energy?

   Ⓐ condensation   Ⓒ warm ocean water

   Ⓑ cold ocean water   Ⓓ tornadoes

2. What specific information does the author include about vortexes?

_____

_____

_____

_____

_____

3. What words does the author use to describe density?

_____

_____

_____

_____

_____

Fiction Text Teacher Notes
Touchdown of the Wrong Kind

	Lesson Steps	Teacher Think Alouds
Ready, Set, Predict!	• Provide the text to students and display a larger version. Read the title aloud. • Have students do a quick and quiet text walk. Ask partners to briefly predict why the author titled the script "Touchdown of a Different Kind" using the following: *I think the author chose this title because _____.*	"The title makes me think of a touchdown in a football game, but after I scanned the text, I saw a lot of references to tornadoes. Perhaps the author is writing about tornadoes touching the ground and that is why she includes the phrase *of the wrong kind.*
Go!	• Ask students to read the script independently to think about the content and to underline unfamiliar words. • Read the script aloud to students. Model changing your voice for each of the characters so students get familiar with them. • Divide the class into groups of four. Assign each group member one role in the script. Have groups read through the script together.	"Do you notice I change my voice for the different characters? Why do you think I do this? Does it help you better understand the text?"
Reread to Clarify	• Have partners reread the text to clarify. Ask them to share the words they underlined in the *Go!* section. • Ask them to work together to clarify the underlined words using the following: *I am unfamiliar with the word _____, so I _____.*	"I am unfamiliar with the word *supercells*, so I read on. The word is clearly defined a few lines down by Mr. Whirl as a *severe thunderstorm.*
Reread to Question	• Tell partners to reread the text to question. Ask them to answer this question using evidence from the text: *Which character helps you the most to understand what a tornado is?* • Open a class discussion on tornadoes. Ask students to build on one anothers' ideas using evidence from the text. • Have students respond to the question and prompts on page 25.	"I notice that some characters seem more certain about their knowledge of tornadoes than others. They are the ones who really help me understand more about tornadoes. For example, when Sonny says, *They start off as regular storms, right?* I'm not sure if the information is correct. When Mr. Whirl says *They sure do*, I know that the information is accurate."
Reread to Summarize and Respond	• Ask students to reread the script to summarize. Invite partners to clearly explain to one another what happens in the script and what a tornado is. • Review the close reading strategies by singing the song on page 128.	

*Note: For more tips, engagement strategies, and fluency options to include in this lesson, see pages 122–128.

Touchdown of the Wrong Kind

by Stephanie Macceca

Mr. Whirl: So, tell me what you already know about tornadoes.

Sonny: Aren't they also called funnels?

Wendy: I've heard them called twisters and whirlwinds.

Mom: A tornado can also be called a wedge, gustnado, landspout, or rope.

Mr. Whirl: What else do you know about tornadoes?

Sonny: They start off as regular storms, right?

Mr. Whirl: They sure do. You kids know about evaporation and condensation, right?

Sonny: Evaporation is when a liquid turns into a gas. It evaporates.

Wendy: Condensation is when a gas turns into a liquid.

Sonny: Or it can turn solid if the air is colder than the freezing point.

Mom: I'm impressed. You two have really been paying attention during science class.

Wendy: Mist, rain, hail, sleet, and snow come from clouds. Clouds are just water vapor moving in the air.

Mr. Whirl: That's right. Sometimes we have severe thunderstorms in Kansas, with lots of clouds.

Sonny: I know that tornadoes occur during severe thunderstorms.

Mr. Whirl: Have you ever heard of supercells?

Wendy: Are supercells like the cells in our body?

Mr. Whirl: A *supercell* is a severe thunderstorm. It can form when the wind changes speed or direction. When the speed, direction, and height change, we get something called wind shear. Wind shears cause the updraft and downdraft that move around, creating a mesocyclone. A supercell with a mesocyclone produces a tornado almost 30 percent of the time.

Touchdown of the Wrong Kind (cont)

Mom: No one is exactly sure how a tornado forms, but we do know this—toward the end of the mesocyclone, in a supercell, we can often see an area of rain-free clouds that are rotating. If the rotating gets stronger, funnel clouds form and become tornadoes when they touch the ground.

Wendy: So, tornadoes have to do with the weather.

Sonny: I think I need to learn more about weather systems.

Wendy: That's a good idea!

• •

"Touchdown of the Wrong Kind" Response

Directions: Reread the script on pages 24–25 to answer each question.

1. What is a supercell?

   Ⓐ a regular storm   Ⓒ a mesocyclone

   Ⓑ a severe thunderstorm   Ⓓ a landspout

2. How does Wendy describe condensation?

   _____

   _____

   _____

   _____

3. How is a mesocyclone created?

   _____

   _____

   _____

   _____

Name:_____ Date: _____

Let's Compare!
Weird Weather!

Directions: Use the information from both texts to create an informational poster about tornadoes and hurricanes. Your poster should be one that can hang in a classroom and educate students about these forms of weird weather. Include diagrams, illustrations, and photos on your poster. Use fun colors and fun facts, too! Complete this outline before you start to help you plan.

Title of poster: _____

Important and fun facts about hurricanes: _____

_____

Important and fun facts about tornadoes:_____

_____

Visuals I plan to include:_____

_____

_____

Sketch the layout of your poster.

Thinking About Extreme Weather!

Directions: Choose at least two of these activities to complete.

Radical Reading

Reread "Severe Storms." What is the most interesting part of the text? What is the most surprising part of the text? Share your thoughts with a partner.

Fun Fluency

Find a few friends to play the different characters in "Touchdown of the Wrong Kind." Assign yourself a role, too! Practice reading the text as a group. Then, perform the text for students in a lower grade. You may even want to wear costumes and make props!

Wonderful Words

List 10 adjectives that describe how you would feel if you saw a hurricane or tornado. Try to be creative and imaginative with your words! Can you think of a word that is more than 10 letters long?

Wacky Writing

Imagine you are living through a tornado or hurricane right now! What are you feeling? What are you seeing and hearing? tweet your experience! Write five tweets (140 characters or less each) telling your followers what you are experiencing. Share your tweets with a partner.

Abraham Lincoln

Theme Summary

Abraham Lincoln was a president for the ages. He kept the Union together during the American Civil War and helped end one of the darkest chapters in American history. With this text pair, students will gain a new appreciation for the nation's sixteenth president. The fiction text is Walt Whitman's popular poem while the nonfiction text explores Lincoln's famous second inaugural address.

Answer Key

"Binding Up the Nation's Wounds" Response (page 31)

1. A. a victory speech

2. The author says the speech *sounded like a sermon*. The evidence the author provides is that Lincoln referenced the Bible and *mentioned God 14 times*.

3. Lincoln helped explain the war and bring the nation together. He *focused on cooperating in the future* and urged *Americans to work together*.

"O Captain! My Captain" Response (page 34)

1. A. a crew member on the ship

2. The narrator describes the captain as having pale, still lips and no pulse.

3. The phrase *for you* is repeated five times. Answers will vary but may include that the poet wants the focus on the captain and therefore repeats the *for you* phrase.

Let's Compare! Memorializing Lincoln (page 35)

Students' obituaries will vary. Check that the obituaries include factual information about Abraham Lincoln's life.

Standards

➡ Determine a theme of a story, drama, or poem from details in the text, including how characters in a story or drama respond to challenges or how the speaker in a poem reflects upon a topic.

➡ Explain how an author uses reasons and evidence to support particular points in a text, identifying which reasons and evidence support which point(s).

➡ Demonstrate understanding of figurative language, word relationships, and nuances in word meanings.

Materials

➡ *Binding Up the Nation's Wounds* (pages 30–31)

➡ *"Binding Up the Nation's Wounds" Response* (page 31)

➡ *O Captain! My Captain!* (page 33)

➡ *"O Captain! My Captain!" Response* (page 34)

➡ *Let's Compare! Memorializing Lincoln* (page 35)

➡ *Thinking About Abraham Lincoln!* (page 36)

➡ pencils

Comparing the Texts

After students complete the lessons for each text, have them work in pairs or groups to reread both texts and complete the *Let's Compare! Memorializing Lincoln* activity page (page 35). Finally, students can work to complete the *Thinking About Abraham Lincoln!* matrix (page 36). The matrix activities allow students to work on the important literacy skills of reading, writing, vocabulary, and fluency.

Binding Up the Nation's Wounds

		Lesson Steps	Teacher Think Alouds
Ready, Set, Predict!		• Tell students that they will read a nonfiction text about President Lincoln. Ask them to use prior knowledge to quickly list at least three things they already know about him. • Have partners share their lists. • Provide the text to students and display a larger version for the class to see.	"Before I begin to read a text, I stop and think of all the things I already know about the topic of the text. This helps me to better understand what I am about to read."
Go!		• Ask students to read the text independently and circle words they find tricky or confusing. Encourage reluctant students by having them circle words that younger students might have trouble with. • Read the text aloud to students. Model fluent reading.	
Reread to Clarify		• Review the difference between figurative and literal meanings of words and phrases. • Have partners reread the text to clarify information. Ask each pair to look at the words or phrases they circled previously to clarify. Have them determine together if any of the phrases are figurative language.	"Many authors use figurative language. This means that words are not meant to have their normal meanings applied. When Lincoln says *bind up the nation's wounds* he does not mean literally dressing soldiers' war wounds. He means healing the nation and bringing the country together."
Reread to Question		• Ask students to reread the text in pairs to question. Have them each identify one point the author makes and write down a question about that point. Then, have them switch papers and underline sentences in the text that provide evidence to support the answers to the questions they received. • Have students respond to the question and prompts on page 31.	"The point I identify is the weather reflected the state of the nation, so my question is 'How was the weather like the state of the nation?' My partner can underline the sentence *The morning had been rainy, but the sun was beginning to peek through the clouds* to help answer my question."
Reread to Summarize and Respond		• Invite students to reread the text to summarize. Ask them to mark the text using the following symbols: + main idea √ details ! cool idea ☺ favorite part	

*Note: For more tips, engagement strategies, and fluency options to include in this lesson, see pages 122–128.

Language Arts Texts

Binding Up the Nation's Wounds

by Stephanie Kuligowski

Abraham Lincoln was re-elected president in November 1864. The Civil War was nearing an end, and Lincoln was making plans to reunite the North and the South.

Lincoln's inauguration was held on the morning of March 4, 1865. The weather reflected the state of the nation. The morning had been rainy, but the sun was beginning to peek through the clouds as the ceremony began. Tens of thousands of people had gathered in the muddy streets of Washington, D.C., for the event.

With a Union win close at hand, the audience probably expected Lincoln to give a victory speech in which he would say that good had triumphed over evil. They probably wanted to hear about the punishments he was planning for the Southern traitors. Instead, Lincoln's speech sounded like a sermon. He referenced the Bible. He mentioned God 14 times. He spoke about the divine purpose of the war. As he saw it, the long and brutal war was God's punishment on the nation for the sin of slavery. The punishment was for both the North and the South. Lincoln explained, ". . . He [God] gives to both North and South this terrible war as the woe due to those by whom the offense [slavery] came."

Instead of demanding punishment for the South, Lincoln urged forgiveness. He quoted the Bible again, saying ". . . but let us judge not, that we be not judged." Lincoln's Reconstruction plan focused on cooperating in the future rather than retaliation for the past.

Lincoln ended his speech by urging Americans to work together to heal the broken nation. He said, "With malice toward none, with charity for all, with firmness in the right as God gives us to see the right, let us strive on to finish the work we are in, to bind up the nation's wounds, to care for him who shall have borne the battle and for his widow and his orphan, to do all which may achieve and cherish a just and lasting peace among ourselves and with all nations."

Binding Up the Nation's Wounds (*cont*)

Like the Gettysburg Address, Lincoln's second inaugural address was short. It contained just over 700 words. In the 10 minutes it took Lincoln to read the address, he captivated his audience. The silent crowd hung on his every word. The famous abolitionist Frederick Douglass wrote, "The whole proceeding was wonderfully quiet, earnest, and solemn." Douglass called Lincoln's address "a sacred effort."

Lincoln believed it was his best speech, and many scholars agree. In his brief statement, Lincoln helped Americans make sense of the terrible war. He turned their attention to the future and inspired them to cooperate to reunite the country.

"Binding Up the Nation's Wounds" Response

Directions: Reread the text on pages 30–31 to answer each question.

1. What was the audience expecting from Lincoln at his second inaugural speech?

    (A) a victory speech

    (B) a speech about Gettysburg

    (C) a speech about Reconstruction

    (D) a speech about Frederick Douglass

2. What does the author say Lincoln's speech sounded like? What evidence does the author provide?

    _____

    _____

    _____

3. What did Lincoln accomplish with his second inaugural speech? What evidence in the text supports this inference?

    _____

    _____

    _____

Fiction Text Teacher Notes
O Captain! My Captain!

	Lesson Steps	Teacher Think Alouds

Ready, Set, Predict!

- Read the title aloud and ask students to predict what the text is about.
- Provide students with the text and display a larger version. Have them skim it. Tell them the poem is about a famous U.S. president. Have students guess which president.

"When I skim the text, it's hard to know who it is talking about. When I look at the image, I know right away that this poem must be about Abraham Lincoln."

Go!

- Have students read the text silently. Ask them to circle the exclamation marks as they read.
- Read the poem aloud to students. Review with students how exclamation marks affect how the poem is read. Pair students and have them practice reading the poem to one another, focusing on the punctuation.

"Listen to how my voice goes up and is more expressive with lines that end in exclamation marks. How does reading the poem fluently change your understanding of the text?"

Reread to Clarify

- Briefly share the meaning and forms of figurative language with students, including metaphors, similes, and personifications.
- Draw students' attention to the line *The ship is safe and sound*. Discuss this metaphor as a class. Explain to students that the ship represents the Union.
- Have students reread the text in small groups to clarify it. Ask them to underline the figurative language that they want clarified.

"Figurative language is the use of words or expressions that mean something different from the basic meaning. For example, Whitman uses the phrase *our fearful trip* as a metaphor for the Civil War. Sometimes figurative language is hard for me. I make sure to read the lines I find confusing twice, or I ask a friend to help me."

Reread to Question

- Remind students that good readers look for themes as they read and question what they read. Ask, "What is the theme of this poem?" Have groups think about this question as they reread the text.
- Have students respond to the question and prompts on page 34.

"As I read the text, I remind myself to think about the theme of the poem. By remembering the theme, I am able to better understand the lines in the poem."

Reread to Summarize and Respond

- Ask students to reread the text to summarize. Have them summarize the last stanza in their own words. Invite them to share their summaries with partners.
- Review the close reading strategies by singing the song on page 128.

*Note: For more tips, engagement strategies, and fluency options to include in this lesson, see pages 122–128.

O Captain! My Captain!

by Walt Whitman

O CAPTAIN! my Captain! our fearful trip is done;
The ship has weathered every rack, the prize we sought is won;
The port is near, the bells I hear, the people all exulting,

While follow eyes the steady keel, the vessel grim and daring:
    But O heart! heart! heart!
      O the bleeding drops of red,
        Where on the deck my Captain lies,
          Fallen cold and dead.

O Captain! my Captain! rise up and hear the bells;

Rise up—for you the flag is flung—for you the bugle trills;
For you bouquets and ribbon'd wreaths for you the shores a-crowding;
For you they call, the swaying mass, their eager faces turning;
    Here Captain! dear father!
      This arm beneath your head;
        It is some dream that on the deck,
          You've fallen cold and dead.

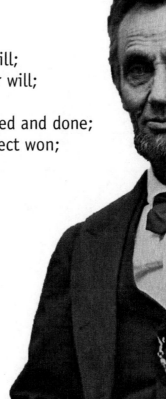

My Captain does not answer, his lips are pale and still;
My father does not feel my arm, he has no pulse nor will;

The ship is anchor'd safe and sound, its voyage closed and done;
From fearful trip, the victor ship, comes in with object won;
    Exult, O shores, and ring, O bells!
      But I, with mournful tread,
        Walk the deck my Captain lies,
          Fallen cold and dead.

Language Arts Texts

"O Captain! My Captain!" Response

Directions: Reread the poem on page 33 to answer each question.

1. Who is the narrator of the poem?

   Ⓐ a crew member on the ship   Ⓒ Confederate soldier

   Ⓑ a Union soldier   Ⓓ the captain

2. How does the narrator describe the captain in the third stanza? Use evidence from the text to support your answer.

   _____

   _____

   _____

   _____

   _____

3. What phrase is repeated five times in the second stanza? Why do you think the poet does this?

   _____

   _____

   _____

   _____

   _____

Let's Compare!

Memorializing Lincoln

Directions: An obituary is an article in a newspaper about the life of someone who has recently died. Reread the two texts. Make a list of all the noteworthy items you learn about Lincoln. Then, use your notes to write an obituary for the fallen president.

****** Special Memorial Edition ******

The National News

VOL. XIV–NO. 4230	WASHINGTON, SATURDAY, APRIL 15, 1865	PRICE: TEN CENTS

LINCOLN SHOT

_____

_____

_____

_____

_____

_____

_____

_____

_____

_____

_____

_____

_____

_____

_____

Name:_____   Date: _____

Thinking About Abraham Lincoln!

Directions: Choose at least two of these activities to complete.

Radical Reading

Reread "Binding Up the Nation's Wounds." Highlight a part of the text that you want to learn more about. Then, conduct some research. Add a few sentences to that part of the text in the margin or at the bottom of the page that tells what you learn.

Fun Fluency

Practice reading "O Captain! My Captain!" by yourself. What tone of voice is appropriate for this poem? Be sure to use the correct tone and pay careful attention to the punctuation and the speed at which you read the poem. When you read it fluently, perform it for your friends or family.

Wonderful Words

If you had to choose just three words to describe President Lincoln, which three words would you choose and why? Provide evidence from the texts. Share your writing with a partner.

Wacky Writing

Whitman's "O Captain! My Captain!" was well received and very popular in its day. How do you feel about Whitman's poem? Imagine you are a poetry critic. Write a review of Whitman's poem. Give two reasons why you like it or do not like it.

Adding Fractions

Theme Summary

Fractions often present challenges for students. It is important that students develop tools and motivation to tackle and solve problems involving fractions. Students will read an encouraging poem about solving math problems with fractions. The nonfiction text will help students learn how to add and subtract fractions in a step-by-step manner.

Standards

➡ Determine a theme of a story, drama, or poem from details in the text, including how characters in a story or drama respond to challenges or how the speaker in a poem reflects upon a topic; summarize the text.

➡ Determine the meaning of general academic and domain-specific words and phrases in a text relevant to a grade 5 topic or subject area.

➡ Solve word problems involving addition of fractions referring to the same whole, including cases of unlike denominators. Use benchmark fractions and number sense of fractions to estimate mentally and assess the reasonableness of answers.

Materials

➡ *Thinking About Different Sizes* (page 39)

➡ *"Thinking About Different Sizes" Response* (page 40)

➡ *Solving Math Problems* (page 42)

➡ *"Solving Math Problems" Response* (page 43)

➡ *Let's Compare! Motivational Math!* (page 44)

➡ *Thinking About Fractions!* (page 45)

➡ pencils

➡ index cards

Comparing the Texts

After students complete the lessons for each text, have them work in pairs or groups to reread both texts and complete the *Let's Compare! Motivational Math!* activity page (page 44). Finally, students can work to complete the *Thinking About Fractions!* matrix (page 45). The matrix activities allow students to work on the important literacy skills of reading, writing, vocabulary, and fluency.

Answer Key

"Thinking About Different Sizes" Response (page 40)

1. A. The fractions have common denominators.

2. The first thing you need to do when adding fractions without common denominators is change the fractions to *an equivalent form*.

3. You do not have to change anything, you just *simply add the numerators* and then *simplify as needed*.

"Solving Math Problems" Response (page 43)

1. C. patience and powers of the mind

2. The author's message is that you can solve any math problem if you put your mind to it. You just need to use your *noodles* or *noggin* and have *patience* and *powers of the mind*.

3. I know this poem is about mathematics because there are mathematical terms used throughout the poem such as *problem, solve, numbers, facts, product, quotient, sum, factorials,* and *answer*.

Let's Compare! Motivational Math! (page 44)

$\frac{1}{2} + \frac{2}{5} = \frac{9}{10}$; Students' songs or poems will vary but should include information for how they got $\frac{9}{10}$ as an answer.

Thinking About Different Sizes

Mathematics Texts

	Lesson Steps	Teacher Think Alouds
Ready, Set, Predict!	• Distribute the text to students and display a larger version of it for the class to see. • Have students scan the text, looking at the problems and illustrations. Ask them to predict why the author would write a text like this using the following: *I think the author wrote this to _____ because _____.*	"Before reading a text, I think about the reason the author wrote the text. Since this text is about adding and subtracting fractions, I think the author wants to teach me something."
Go!	• Tell students to read the text silently and think about the content. Ask them to underline all the mathematical terms. • Read the text aloud as students follow along. Model fluent reading. • Direct partners to perform alternate readings of the text, switching between paragraphs and steps. Remind students to practice good fluency while reading aloud.	"Notice how I read the text clearly and accurately. I do not rush through the text and I keep a consistent pace. I also pay close attention to the mathematical signs and numbers so that I read them accurately."
Reread to Clarify	• Invite pairs to reread the text to clarify information. Have them circle mathematical terms they found tricky or confusing. • Ask pairs to use two different strategies to clarify the terms they circled (e.g., *read on, ask a friend*) • Have one or two students share their words and strategies with the class.	"One tricky word is *denominator*. I ask a friend what the word means and she reminds me that it is the bottom number in a fraction."
Reread to Question	• Tell groups to reread the text to question. Challenge them to write math problems like the ones in the text. Then, have groups swap their problems with other groups and solve them using the correct steps. • Have students respond to the question and prompts on page 40.	
Reread to Summarize and Respond	• Instruct students to reread the text to summarize. Tell them to make a "cheat sheet" or study guide on index cards. The information on the cards should help them remember how to add fractions with and without common denominators. • Invite students to swap index cards with partners to see if they have any tips or tricks that they can add to their own cards.	

Thinking About Different Sizes

by Lori Barker

Cade is in a marching band in a parade. After marching four-eighths of a mile, his sheet music blows away, so Cade marches without his music the remaining three-eighths of a mile. What was the total distance of the parade route?

Fractions with Common Denominators

Some fractions, like the ones above, have common denominators. This means the denominators are the same. It is easy to add or subtract these fractions. Just add or subtract the numerators. Keep the denominator the same and simplify as needed. To find the length of the parade route, you simply add 4 and 3 to get the numerator, and you keep the same denominator. So, the total length is $\frac{7}{8}$ of a mile.

Fractions Without Common Denominators

Some fractions do not have common denominators. But we can add and subtract them, too. First, the fractions must be changed to an equivalent form. Then the steps you know can be followed. Let's add $\frac{1}{2} + \frac{1}{3}$.

Step 1: Draw a picture that shows each fraction.

One-half of this rectangle is shaded.

One-third of this rectangle is shaded.

Step 2: Divide the rows and columns. Each should have the same number and size of pieces.

The second rectangle has three rows.
Draw three equal rows in the first rectangle.
You divide each column into thirds.

The first rectangle has two columns.
Draw two equal columns in the second rectangle.
You divide each row into halves.

Step 3: The two rectangles should each have pieces of equal size. Now, combine them into one rectangle: $\frac{1}{2} + \frac{1}{3} = \frac{3}{6} + \frac{2}{6} = \frac{5}{6}$

Mathematics Texts

"Thinking About Different Sizes" Response

Directions: Reread the text on page 39 to answer each question.

1. Why is finding out the distance of the parade route easy?

   Ⓐ The fractions have common denominators.

   Ⓑ The fractions do not have common denominators.

   Ⓒ You have to multiply the fractions.

   Ⓓ The fractions are the same.

2. What do you need to do first to add fractions that do not have common denominators? Use evidence from the text to support your answer.

   _____

   _____

   _____

   _____

   _____

3. How do you add fractions if the denominators are the same? Use evidence from the text to support your answer.

   _____

   _____

   _____

   _____

   _____

Fiction Text Teacher Notes
Solving Math Problems

	Lesson Steps	Teacher Think Alouds
Ready, Set, Predict!	• Provide the text to students and display a larger version for the class to see. Have students do a quick and quiet text walk. • Ask students to predict the author's audience. Have partners discuss their predictions using the following: *I think the author wrote this for _____ (what audience) because _____?*	"Thinking about the author's audience can help me figure out the author's purpose for writing and can help me to better understand the text."
Go!	• Have students read the text independently to get a basic understanding of the content. Ask them to underline text that points to the author's audience and her purpose for writing it. • Read the poem aloud to students. Model fluent reading.	
Reread to Clarify 	• Tell partners to reread the text to clarify it. Ask them to circle words they think younger students may find tricky. • Direct each pair to choose a strategy to help clarify their circled words. Ask volunteers to share their words and strategies with the class using the following: *The word _____ is tricky because _____ so we _____.*	"The word *noodle* is tricky because it is a food item. I would explain to a younger student that here the word *noodle* means 'brains' or 'head.'"
Reread to Question	• Invite partners to reread the poem to question. • Tell partners to think about the main idea of the poem. Direct them to ask questions about the main idea to one another such as *What is one thing we can use to solve math problems?* • Have students respond to the question and prompts on page 43.	"Identifying the main theme in a poem helps me to better understand what I am reading. I see words such as *noodles, noggins,* and *mind* as well as *numbers, sum,* and *factorials.* I think the main theme in this poem may be using your mind to solve math problems."
Reread to Summarize and Respond	• Instruct students to reread the text to summarize. Ask them to illustrate the poem. Have them share their illustrations with partners. • Ask students if this poem inspires them and makes them believe they can solve all math problems. Have students explain their reasoning to partners.	

*Note: For more tips, engagement strategies, and fluency options to include in this lesson, see pages 122–128.

Name:_____ Date:_____

Solving Math Problems

by Sarah Kartchner Clark

We never met a problem
That we couldn't solve.
We just use our noodles—
That's all we need involve.

No matter what the numbers,
No matter what the facts,
We just use our noggins
And the problem we attack.

We can find the product,
The quotient, or the sum.
We can find factorials
Until the job is done.

There's never been an answer
That we couldn't find.
All it takes is patience
And the powers of the mind.

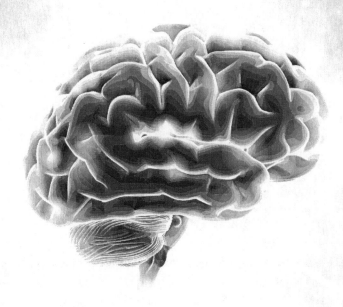

"Solving Math Problems" Response

Directions: Reread the poem on page 42 to answer each question.

1. In the last stanza, what does the speaker of the poem say it takes to find an answer to a math problem?

   Ⓐ determination

   Ⓒ patience and powers of the mind

   Ⓑ motivation

   Ⓓ the quotient or the sum

2. What is the message the author of the poem is trying to get across? Use evidence from the text to support your answer.

   _____

   _____

   _____

   _____

   _____

3. How do you know this poem is about mathematics? Use evidence from the text to support your answer.

   _____

   _____

   _____

   _____

   _____

Let's Compare!
Motivational Math!

Directions: Reread both texts. Solve the problem below by completing the steps. Then, write a motivational poem, song, or rap on a separate sheet of paper describing how you solved the problem. It should explain how you found the answer and should encourage others to do the same.

$$\frac{1}{2} + \frac{2}{5} =$$

Step 1: Draw a picture that shows each fraction.

Step 2: Divide the rows and columns. Each should have the same number and size of pieces.

Step 3: Combine them into one rectangle.

Thinking About Fractions!

Directions: Choose at least two of these activities to complete.

Radical Reading

Reread "Thinking About Different Sizes." Make flash cards to help you remember the mathematical terms used in the text.

Fun Fluency

Practice reading "Solving Math Problems" with a partner. Read every other stanza of the poem with your partner. Practice until the poem sounds seamless. Next, make up a fun or silly dance to go with the poem. You may even want to make props. Then, perform the poem for family or friends.

Wonderful Words

The poem "Solving Math Problems" is motivational. It inspires students to believe in themselves and use their skills to solve math problems. How many uplifting or encouraging words can you think of? Can you think of one for each letter in the alphabet? Give it a try!

Wacky Writing

We all use math in the real world. Think of a time when you have had to add or subtract a fraction outside of school and homework. Write a short paragraph about it. For example, have you ever had to share food with a group of friends?

Theme Summary

Is it right, acute, or obtuse? Maybe it's an equilateral, isosceles, or scalene? Triangles can be tricky unless you know their specific attributes. In this pair of texts, students will learn all about triangles. They will read *a cute* and clever reader's theater featuring two-dimensional shapes and a nonfiction text featuring the various types of triangles. This unit is sure to be just *right* for your students!

Answer Key

"Understanding Triangles" Response (page 49)

1. D. 180°

2. The measure of each angle in an equilateral triangle is 60°, because all three sides and all three angles in an equilateral triangle are *equal,* and all angles in any triangle add up to 180°.

3. A right triangle has one and only one right angle that measures 90°. Typically a little box is placed in the corner of the right angle in a right triangle.

"You're Cute!" Response (page 52)

1. B. No, acute.

2. There are six types of triangles referenced in the text: acute, obtuse, right, equilateral, isosceles (I saw Sally's) and scalene.

3. Triangle sighs because she is frustrated that the other shapes are calling her *cute* instead of *acute.* At the end of the text, Square calls a scalene triangle *acute,* further frustrating Triangle.

Let's Compare! Triangle Trading Cards (page 53)

Students' cards will vary. Check that the facts on the backs of the cards match the triangle pictures on the fronts of the cards.

Standards

➡ Quote accurately from a text when explaining what the text says explicitly and when drawing inferences from the text.

➡ Determine the meaning of general academic and domain-specific words and phrases in a text relevant to a grade 5 topic or subject area.

➡ Understand that attributes belonging to a category of two-dimensional figures also belong to all subcategories of that category.

➡ Understand the defining properties of triangles.

Materials

➡ *Understanding Triangles* (page 48)

➡ *"Understanding Triangles" Response* (page 49)

➡ *You're Cute!* (page 51)

➡ *"You're Cute!" Response* (page 52)

➡ *Let's Compare! Triangle Trading Cards* (page 53)

➡ *Thinking About Triangles!* (page 54)

➡ pencils

➡ highlighters

➡ index cards

➡ drawing paper

Comparing the Texts

After students complete the lessons for each text, have them work in pairs or groups to reread both texts and complete the *Let's Compare! Triangle Trading Cards* (page 53). Finally, students can work independently to complete the *Thinking About Triangles!* matrix (page 54). The matrix activities allow students to work on the important literacy skills of reading, writing, vocabulary, and fluency.

Nonfiction Text Teacher Notes
Understanding Triangles

	Lesson Steps	Teacher Think Alouds
Ready, Set, Predict!	• Read the title of the text aloud to students. Ask them to predict what the text will be about and why the author wrote it. • Have students think-pair-share any prior knowledge they have about triangles.	
Go!	• Provide the text to students and display a larger version. Invite them to read the text independently to get a basic understanding of it and to circle words that they want to know more about. • Read the text aloud. Model fluent reading. • Discuss with students how reading fluently helps convey meaning and promotes understanding.	"There is a lot of information in this text. I make sure to read it slowly and clearly. This makes the text easier to understand for those who are listening."
Reread to Clarify	• Have students reread the text independently to clarify it and to underline sentences that they had to read twice to understand. • Tell students to work in small groups to help one another clarify the parts of the text they underlined.	
Reread to Question	• Ask partners to reread the text to question. Have them highlight 10 words from the text that they think are important mathematical vocabulary words. Have them create glossaries for those 10 words. • Instruct partners to write questions that can be answered using their glossaries. Have pairs switch glossaries and questions with other pairs to answer the questions. • Have students respond to the question and prompts on page 49.	"In my glossary, I included the definition for a right triangle. My question about this type of triangle is 'What does a right triangle measure?'"
Reread to Summarize and Respond	• Tell students to reread the text to summarize. Ask them to describe the most important points in the text to partners. • Invite volunteers to share their points with the class.	"Summarizing the text by describing the content in my own words helps ensure that I truly understand the text."

*Note: For more tips, engagement strategies, and fluency options to include in this lesson, see pages 122–128.

Name:_____   Date: _____

Understanding Triangles

Adapted from a piece by Lori Barker

A triangle is a closed two-dimensional figure with three line segments for its sides. It is a three-sided polygon. The sides meet at three points called *vertices*. Each vertex forms an angle with two of the sides. The word *triangle* means "three angles." If you add up the measures of the three angles of a triangle, they will always total 180°.

There are two ways to name triangles: by their angles or by their sides. This is important to know. It helps explain the differences among triangles.

A right angle measures exactly 90°. If a triangle has a right angle, it is called a right triangle. A triangle cannot have more than one right angle. For people to know an angle is a right angle, you need to put a little box in the corner of the right angle.

If a triangle has three acute angles, it is called an acute triangle. Each angle is less than 90°.

If a triangle has one obtuse angle, it is called an obtuse triangle. An obtuse angle is greater than 90°. A triangle cannot have more than one obtuse angle.

An equilateral triangle has three equal sides and three equal angles. All three angles in an equilateral triangle are 60°.

An isosceles triangle has only two equal sides. This special kind of triangle also has two equal angles. The angles opposite the equal sides are the same measure.

A scalene triangle has no equal sides. These triangles also have no equal angles.

Triangles can be used in architecture. They are strong shapes. You see them used in rooftops. You see them used in parts of floors and ceilings. You even see them used in bridges!

Name:_____ Date:_____

"Understanding Triangles" Response

Directions: Reread the text on page 48 to answer each question.

1. If you add the three angles of a triangle, what will always be the total?

   Ⓐ 90º   Ⓒ 360º

   Ⓑ 60º   Ⓓ 180º

2. What is the measure of each angle in an equilateral triangle? How do you know? Use evidence from the text.

   _____

   _____

   _____

   _____

   _____

3. Describe and draw a right triangle.

   _____

   _____

   _____

   _____

   _____

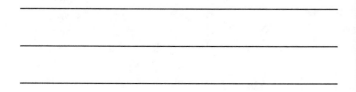

Fiction Text Teacher Notes
You're Cute!

	Lesson Steps	Teacher Think Alouds
Ready, Set, Predict!	• Distribute the text to students and display a larger version. Tell them to do a quick and quiet text walk. • Ask partners to discuss how they think the text is organized using the following: *I think the text is organized like _____ because _____.*	
Go! 	• Have students read the text independently to think about the content and to put asterisks (*) next to words related to triangles. • Read the text aloud to students. Model fluent reading using punctuation. • Divide the class into five groups. Assign each group one part of the reader's theater. Read through the script as a class with students reading their assigned parts.	"Listen to how my voice goes higher at the ends of the lines that have question marks. Can you hear the excitement in my voice when I read a line with an exclamation mark?"
Reread to Clarify 	• Read the phrase *I saw Sally's puppy* aloud. Ask students what it has to do with triangles. • Ask groups to reread the script and underline words they think younger students wouldn't understand. Have groups work together to clarify their underlined words.	"There are six types of triangles: right, acute, obtuse, equilateral, scalene, and isosceles. I notice that isosceles isn't mentioned in the text. I reread the text and realize that *I saw Sally's* is actually referencing *isosceles* in a different and fun way."
Reread to Question	• Tell students to reread the text to question. Provide pairs with index cards. Ask them to write questions that can be answered using the text. • Instruct pairs to get together, exchange questions, and try to answer the questions they receive. Students must identify where they find the answers in the text. • Have students respond to the question and prompts on page 52.	"I take my time to think about my question. I want to make sure that it can be answered using evidence from the text. For example, my question is, Why does the triangle keep responding *no, acute*? This helps me remember that the triangle in the poem is trying to tell the others that is an acute triangle."
Reread to Summarize and Respond	• Provide students with drawing paper. Have them fold the paper in half horizontally. Then, fold one end into the middle and then the other. This will create six even squares. • Invite students to reread the text to summarize. Ask them to draw comics to represent the script. Have them add speech bubbles to their comics and share them with partners.	

You're Cute!

Circle: You're cute!

Triangle: No, acute.

Rectangle: How obtuse!

Triangle: No, acute.

Diamond: I think you're right.

Triangle: No, acute.

Square: What's going on here? (*noticing Triangle*) Hey, you're cute!

Triangle: No, acute.

Circle: That's just wrong.

Triangle: No, acute.

Rectangle: Are you trying to be difficult?

Triangle: No, acute.

Diamond: Whatever.

Triangle: No, acute.

Square: Well, it's all equilateral to me.

Triangle: No, acute.

Circle: Look, I don't think you're so cute anymore.

Triangle: No, acute.

Rectangle: I saw Sally's puppy, and it sure was cute.

Triangle: No, acute.

Diamond: You don't have to be so edgy.

Triangle: No, acute!

Square: Let's go talk to that scalene triangle. You know, I think she might be acute.

Triangle: Sigh.

"You're Cute!" Response

Directions: Reread the script on page 51 to answer each question.

1. What is the triangle's repeated response?

   (A) Sigh.

   (B) No, acute.

   (C) Whatever.

   (D) No, I think you're right.

2. How many types of triangles are referenced in the text? List them.

   _____

   _____

   _____

   _____

   _____

3. Why does Triangle sigh at the end of the text? Support your answer with references from the text.

   _____

   _____

   _____

   _____

   _____

Let's Compare!

Triangle Trading Cards

Directions: Reread the texts. Use them to help you create fun and informative triangle trading cards. On one side of each card, draw the triangle in the form of a superhero, sports star, or any other fun figure you would like. On the back of each card, list all the "stats" or examples of the type of triangle drawn on the front.

Mathematics Texts

Thinking About Triangles!

Directions: Choose at least two of these activities to complete.

Radical Reading

Fold a sheet of paper in half. On the left side, write a list of the six types of triangles described in the text. As you reread "Understanding Triangles," list all the facts you learn about each triangle on the right side.

Fun Fluency

"You're Cute!" is a fun skit to perform. Gather up some friends and practice reading the script fluently. Try reading it quickly and slowly. Which sounds better? Make some puppets using craft sticks and construction paper. Then, perform the script for your class.

Wonderful Words

The root word *tri-* means "three." So the word *triangle* means "three angles." Think of words with *tri-* in them. Write them down. Then, write the meaning of each word.

Wacky Writing

Imagine you are a news reporter. Interview the triangle from the "You're Cute!" script. What questions would you ask her? How would she respond?

Unit 6 Overview
The Metric System

Theme Summary

Did you know that the metric system is a result of the French Revolution over 200 years ago? Did you know it is used in every country in the world except three? This pair of texts will get students thinking about the metric system and conversions. A fun fictional poem about this measurement system is paired with a nonfiction text explaining its history and how it works.

Standards

➠ Quote accurately from a text when explaining what the text says explicitly and when drawing inferences from the text.

➠ Convert among different-sized standard measurement units within a given measurement system, and use these conversions in solving multi-step, real world problems.

➠ Solve problems involving units of measurement and convert answers to a larger or smaller unit within the same system.

Materials

➠ *The Metric System and The French Revolution* (page 57)

➠ *"The Metric System and The French Revolution" Response* (page 58)

➠ *Metric Mania* (page 60)

➠ *"Metric Mania" Response* (page 61)

➠ *Let's Compare! Metric System Challenge* (page 62)

➠ *Thinking About the Metric System!* (page 63)

➠ pencils

➠ index cards

➠ highlighters

➠ online resources

Comparing the Texts

After students complete the lessons for each text, have them work in pairs or groups to reread both texts and complete the *Let's Compare! Metric System Challenge* activity page (page 62). Finally, students can work to complete the *Thinking About the Metric System!* matrix (page 63). The matrix activities allow students to work on the important literacy skills of reading, writing, vocabulary, and fluency.

Answer Key

"The Metric System and the French Revolution" Response (page 58)

1. D. 1799

2. The French wanted a new system because the old system was confusing with its *mix of weights and measures*. The French wanted a new system that would be easy to learn and use.

3. The French decided that decimals were better than fractions because they were easier to add, subtract, multiply, and divide.

"Metric Mania" Response (page 61)

1. B. It consists of units of ten and decimals.

2. The author includes the line because she wants the reader to know where the metric system came from.

3. The focus of the third stanza is what the metric system can do. It can measure length, mass, capacity, and volume easily and quickly. It goes with the theme of the metric system being simple to use and understand.

Let's Compare! Metric System Challenge (page 62)

1. France; Students should draw French flags.

2. 5,000 meters; 5 × 1,000

3. French Academy of Science; Students' seals will vary.

Nonfiction Text Teacher Notes
The Metric System and the French Revolution

	Lesson Steps	Teacher Think Alouds
Ready, Set, Predict!	• Read the title of the text aloud to students. Ask them to pair-share any prior knowledge they have about the metric system. Can they name any units of measurement used in the system? If so, list these on the board. • Most students will not know very much about the French Revolution. It may be helpful to briefly provide them with some background information about the revolution before they begin reading.	"Knowing background information on complex topics that are in texts helps me better understand the texts. To gain background knowledge, I might ask a teacher or do some research on the Internet."
Go!	• Distribute the text to students and display a larger version. Have them read it independently and silently to get a basic understanding of the content and to circle any words that they find interesting or unusual. • Read the text aloud as students follow along. Model fluent reading.	
Reread to Clarify	• Have partners reread the text to clarify. Ask them to place question marks in the margin of the text next to any part that they are having trouble understanding. • Tell partners to clarify the parts of the text they labeled with question marks.	
Reread to Question	• Distribute an index card to each student. Direct small groups to reread the text to question. Have each member write a question on the index card. One student will read his or her question. The other group members will highlight where the answer to the question is found in the text. • Have students respond to the question and prompts on page 58.	"I am having trouble with the sentence *It is one ten-millionth of the distance from the* equator *to the North Pole*. I look up *equator* in the dictionary because I don't know what it is. This helps to clarify the sentence."
Reread to Summarize and Respond	• Tell students to reread the text to summarize. Invite them to write brief *first*, *next*, *then*, and *finally* paragraphs. • Ask students to share their summaries with partners.	"Before I write my summary, I am going to reread the text and mark the numbers 1–4 next to the important parts. This will help me remember the order the events occur in."

*Note: For more tips, engagement strategies, and fluency options to include in this lesson, see pages 122–128.

The Metric System and the French Revolution

The metric system is used around the world. (Just the United States, Liberia, and Myanmar do not use it.) But few people know that it came from the French Revolution.

In the 1790s, the French people rebelled. They removed the king from his throne. New rulers took charge. They wanted to get rid of the old ways. France had a mix of weights and measures. There was more than one unit for weight, distance, and volume. All of them were used at the same time! (This was true for most nations at that time.) People were confused.

The new leaders asked the French Academy of Science to help. They were asked to make a new measurement system. The best minds in France were put to the task. The measurements should be easy to learn. They must be easy to use. The new system would be based on the number 10. Each unit would be made up of 10 smaller units. This let decimals be used. Decimals are better than fractions. They are easier to add. They are easier to subtract. They are easier to multiply and divide, too.

Members of France's Academy of Science came up with the metric system. They used Earth itself to set the new measures. First they set the size of one meter. It is one ten-millionth of the distance from the equator to the North Pole. *Meter* is from the Greek word *metro*. It means "to measure."

The scientists liked Greek and Latin prefixes. They used them for the unit names. *Kilo* means "1,000." So one kilometer is 1,000 meters. It is used as a measure of distance (like miles). *Milli* means "one-thousandth." A millimeter is one-thousandth ($\frac{1}{1000}$) of a meter. It is used for tiny measures (like parts of an inch).

France adopted the system. They started to use it in 1799. In 1875, a group of men held a meeting. They wanted to set up worldwide standards. They chose the metric system. Now representatives from 40 nations meet every six years. They talk about possible changes to the system.

"The Metric System and the French Revolution" Response

Directions: Reread the text on page 57 to answer each question.

1. When did France first start using the metric system?

   Ⓐ 1790

   Ⓑ 1875

   Ⓒ 1980

   Ⓓ 1799

2. Why did the French want a new measurement system?

   _____

   _____

   _____

   _____

   _____

3. Why did the French decide to use decimals instead of fractions?

   _____

   _____

   _____

   _____

   _____

Fiction Text Teacher Notes

Metric Mania

	Lesson Steps	Teacher Think Alouds
Ready, Set, Predict!	• Read the title of the poem and the first two lines aloud to students. • Ask partners to briefly predict the theme of the poem using the following: *I think this poem is about _____ because _____.*	
Go!	• Provide the text to students and display a larger version to model. Have students read the poem independently to begin to understand the content. Ask them to circle pairs of rhyming words. • After they finish reading and circling, ask partners to discuss whether their predictions about the theme are correct. • Choral read the poem with students.	"Do you notice that the pairs of rhyming words are at the ends of the lines? For example, in the last stanza, the first two lines end in *equate* and *great*, and the second two lines end with *learn* and *turn*. This is called an AABB rhyming pattern."
Reread to Clarify	• Have students reread the poem in pairs to clarify. Tell them to imagine reciting this poem to younger students. Ask them to underline any words or phrases that they think younger students might have trouble understanding. • Tell partners to work together to clarify the underlined parts using the following: _____ *(word or phrase) is tricky, so we _____ (e.g., reread, read on, ask a friend).*	*"The people there took a stance* is tricky, so we look *stance* up in a dictionary. It means 'a publicly stated opinion.' We ask a friend and she tells us it is a reference to the French Revolution in which the peasants stood up for themselves and wanted to make changes in France."
Reread to Question	• Instruct students to remain in their pairs and reread the poem to question. Ask them to highlight details that tell about the theme. Then, ask partners to create and ask questions to each other about their highlighted parts. • Have students respond to the question and prompts on page 61.	
Reread to Summarize and Respond	• Invite students to reread the poem to summarize. Have them write one-sentence summaries of the poem. • Ask students to select their favorite stanzas and mark them with asterisks (*). Invite partners to share their reasons for choosing the stanzas.	"Before I write my one-sentence summary, I reread the text and think about what the main idea is. The poem revolves around the metric system, so I will make sure to mention the metric system in my summary."

*Note: For more tips, engagement strategies, and fluency options to include in this lesson, see pages 122–128.

Metric Mania

There's a system that is metric,
it is anything but hectic;
Units of ten and decimals,
It's known for being simple.

It has its beginnings in France,
the people there took a stance;
They developed this new system,
masses around the world listened.

It evaluates length and mass,
efficiently and super fast;
It can measure capacity,
Or compute volume rapidly.

1,000 meters does equate
to 1 kilometer, it's great!
Super easy and fun to learn,
start converting now; it's your turn!

"Metric Mania" Response

Directions: Reread the poem on page 60 to answer each question.

1. Why is the metric system known for being simple?

   Ⓐ It can be used with calculators.   Ⓒ It's French.

   Ⓑ It consists of units of ten   Ⓓ It uses fractions.
      and decimals.

2. Why do you think the author includes the line *It has its beginnings in France*?

   _____

   _____

   _____

   _____

   _____

3. What is the focus of the third stanza? How does this focus relate to the overall theme of the poem?

   _____

   _____

   _____

   _____

   _____

Name:_____ Date:_____

Let's Compare!

Metric System Challenge

Directions: Reread both texts. Use them and the Internet to help you complete the challenge.

1. In what country did the metric system begin? Draw a picture of the flag of that country.

   _____

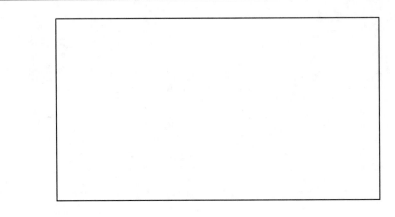

2. If you ran 5 kilometers, how many meters did you run? How did you find the answer? Show your work and the answer in the space below.

3. Which organization did the French ask for help in making the new measurement system? Write the name of the academy on the line below, and then create a seal for the academy.

   _____

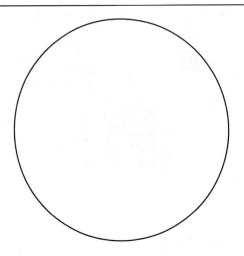

#51361—Close Reading with Paired Texts   © Shell Education

Thinking About the Metric System!

Directions: Choose at least two of these activities to complete.

Radical Reading

Reread "The Metric System and the French Revolution." List the following:

1. Something you did not know

2. Something you already knew

3. Something you want to learn more about

Fun Fluency

Practice reading the poem several times. Remember to pause between stanzas and emphasize the rhyming words. Use a fun voice, too! When you feel ready, perform the poem in front of your family.

Wonderful Words

There are many units of measurement that you can use to measure length, weight, volume, and temperature. How many units of measurement can you think of? List as many as you can in five minutes!

Wacky Writing

Some people in the United States want to switch to the metric system. Others do not. What do you think the United States should do? Write a blog entry stating your opinion and why you feel this way.

Stars

Theme Summary

Twinkle, twinkle, blue supergiant star; how I wonder what you are. Did you know that the billions of stars in our galaxy are grouped by size, mass, and color? In this stellar pair of texts, your all-star students will explore those little twinkles in the sky.

Answer Key

"Classifying Stars" Response (page 67)

1. B. yellow-white star

2. The author compares the color of stars to a campfire. He does this to help the reader better understand how temperature determines a star's color.

3. Yellow stars burn faster than red stars because they have so much mass they burn their fuel faster.

"Shooting Stars" Response (page 70)

1. C. they shoot off through the night like rockets

2. The author is searching and trying to find the falling star that *seemed* to have slipped out of the sky.

3. By *chip* the author means a piece of the falling/shooting star.

Let's Compare! Map of the Stars (page 71)

Students' graphic organizers will vary. Check that the facts students write reflect the main idea in the center of the star.

Standards

➠ Determine the meaning of words and phrases as they are used in a text, including figurative language such as metaphors and similes.

➠ Determine two or more main ideas of a text and explain how they are supported by key details; summarize the text.

➠ Know that astronomical objects in space are massive in size and are separated from one another by vast distances.

Materials

➠ *Classifying Stars* (pages 66–67)

➠ *"Classifying Stars" Response* (page 67)

➠ *Shooting Stars* (page 69)

➠ *"Shooting Stars" Response* (page 70)

➠ *Let's Compare! Map of the Stars* (page 71)

➠ *Thinking About Stars!* (page 72)

➠ pencils

➠ highlighters

➠ paper

Comparing the Texts

After students complete the lessons for each text, have them work in pairs or groups to reread both texts and complete the *Let's Compare! Map of the Stars* activity page (page 71). Finally, students can work to complete the *Thinking About Stars!* matrix (page 72). The matrix activities allow students to work on the important literacy skills of reading, writing, vocabulary, and fluency.

Nonfiction Text Teacher Notes
Classifying Stars

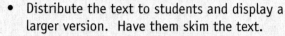

		Lesson Steps	Teacher Think Alouds
	**Ready, Set, Predict!**	• Distribute the text to students and display a larger version. Have them skim the text. • Ask students to predict what they will learn by reading this text using the following: *I think I will learn about _____ because _____.*	"I know the word *classify* means 'to arrange into groups.' I think I will learn about how to group stars because of the title."
	Go!	• Tell students to read the text independently to think about the content and to underline the different ways to group or classify stars. • Read the text aloud. Model fluent reading and pacing. Ask students to raise their hands when you read a part they underlined. • Write the different ways to group stars on the board (*size, color,* and *mass*).	
	**Reread to Clarify**	• Invite students to reread the text in pairs to clarify. Ask them to circle any science-related words they want to clarify. • Have partners discuss with another pair the various strategies they could use to clarify the circled words. Have the pairs work together to then clarify the words.	"I have trouble with the word *supergiant,* so I break the word into two parts, *super* and *giant.* I know that *super* can mean 'very or extremely.' And, I know that *giant* means 'large.' I put the two together and am able to understand the word."
	**Reread to Question**	• Remind students of the three ways stars are grouped. Have students reread the text independently to question. Ask them to highlight key details that explain the three groups. Then, ask students to create questions to go with the key details. • Invite student volunteers to share their questions with the class. • Have students respond to the question and prompts on page 67.	"My question is 'What evidence does this author use to show that color is a way to group stars?' To answer this question using the text, I will highlight the phrases *There are red, orange, yellow, white, and blue stars* and *Their temperatures determine their color.*"
	**Reread to Summarize and Respond**	• Ask students to reread the text to verbally summarize the main points to partners. • Tell students to draw stars in the margins by the most surprising facts in the text and share them with partners.	

***Note:** For more tips, engagement strategies, and fluency options to include in this lesson, see pages 122–128.*

Science Texts

Classifying Stars

by Jack L. Roberts

Have you ever tried to count all of the stars in the sky? How many did you count? The naked eye can see only about 2,000 stars in the sky at any one time. But there are many, many more stars in the universe. In fact, scientists guess that there are more than 100 billion stars just in our galaxy! Our sun is just one of them.

Our sun is considered an average star. It is very much like other stars in the universe. All these average stars closely match in mass and are made of mostly hydrogen and helium.

Stars are often grouped. They can be grouped by size. Some stars are much larger than our sun and are known as supergiants. The red supergiant, Betelgeuse, is thought to be 700 times larger than the sun. Smaller stars are known as dwarf stars.

Mass is another way stars are grouped. Some stars are 30 times more massive than our sun, while others may be only a tenth of the sun's mass.

Color is yet another way to compare stars. There are red, orange, yellow, white, and blue stars. Their temperatures determine their colors. Red stars are the coolest, while blue stars are the hottest. You can see something much like this in a campfire. The red embers are the coolest parts of the fire. The blue flames are the hottest. Over a star's life, it may change size and color as it gets older.

Yellow-white stars are hotter than red stars. They look yellow because they have a medium temperature. Our sun is an example of a yellow-white star. It looks yellow from here on Earth. But from space, the light of the sun appears white.

The sun's mass is about 330,000 times the mass of Earth. Yet, the sun is one of the least massive stars among the stars in this category. With so much mass, yellow stars burn their fuel faster than red stars. They will not live as long as red stars. Yellow-white stars live only about 10 billion years. Scientists say that our sun has already lived 5 billion years. So, it still has a long time before it burns out.

Classifying Stars (cont)

Blue stars are the most massive and the hottest of all stars. These stars are rare. There are only an estimated 1 to 3 million blue supergiant stars. Their mass is 100 to 150 times the mass of the sun. Because blue stars are so huge, they burn their fuel more quickly than other stars. The life cycle of a blue star is only a few million years. Eta Carinae is an example of a blue star. It is about 8,000 light years from Earth and is about 2.6 million years old. Scientists expect this big star to become a supernova—a star that ends its life in a huge explosion. They think this will happen within the next 100,000 years!

"Classifying Stars" Response

Directions: Reread the text on pages 66–67 to answer each question.

1. What type of star is our sun?

   Ⓐ blue star   Ⓒ red star

   Ⓑ yellow-white star   Ⓓ white star

2. What does the author compare the colors of stars to? Why does he do this?

   _____

   _____

   _____

   _____

3. Why do yellow stars burn faster than red stars? Support your answer with text evidence.

   _____

   _____

   _____

   _____

Fiction Text Teacher Notes

Shooting Stars

Lesson Steps	Teacher Think Alouds

Ready, Set, Predict!

- Read the title of the poem aloud.
- Ask partners to quickly predict all the possible topics this text could be about.
- Distribute the text to students and display a larger version.

Go!

- Have students read the poem silently and independently to get a basic understanding of the content. Ask them to underline the longest words in the poem.
- Read the poem aloud to students. Model good phrasing and expression.

Reread to Clarify

- Ask students to reread the poem in pairs to clarify and to circle any words or phrases they think a young child would have trouble understanding.
- Have students work in their pairs to clarify the circled words in a way younger children would understand.

"A young child may not know what *socket* means. I would read them the different definitions for the word from a dictionary. I would then explain which definition the author is referring to and show a picture of the type of socket."

Reread to Question

- Discuss the difference between the figurative and literal use of words. Explain why authors use figurative language in poetry. Answer any questions students may have about figurative language.
- Ask partners to reread the poem to question. Have them ask one another questions about the figurative language such as: *What are two examples of figurative language used in this poem? Why does the author use this language?*
- Have students respond to the question and prompts on page 70.

"I know that poets use figurative language such as metaphors and similes to help me visualize or create images in my head. This helps me better understand the poem. For example, the poet uses the simile *When stars get loosened/ in their sockets/they shoot off through/the night like rockets.* This helps me really see and understand what the shooting stars look like."

Reread to Summarize and Respond

- Provide partners with white paper. Tell students to reread the text to summarize. Ask them to draw pictures that sequence the events in the poem.

"Before I draw my pictures, I reread the text and look at the sequence of events."

Shooting Stars

Science Texts

by Aileen Fisher

When stars get loosened
in their sockets,
they shoot off through
the night like rockets.
But though I stay
and watch their trip
and search where they
have seemed to slip,
I never yet have found a chip
to carry in my pockets.

Name:_____ Date: _____

"Shooting Stars" Response

Directions: Reread the poem on page 69 to answer each question.

1. What simile does the author use?

   Ⓐ stars get loosened in
   their sockets

   Ⓒ they shoot off through the
   night like rockets

   Ⓑ where they have seemed to slip

   Ⓓ none of the above

2. What does the author mean when she says *search where they/have seemed to slip*?

   _____

   _____

   _____

   _____

   _____

3. What is the author referring to when she uses the word *chip*?

   _____

   _____

   _____

   _____

   _____

Let's Compare!
Map of the Stars

Directions: Reread both texts. Write the main idea about stars in the center of the star. In each point of the star, write a fact you learned about stars.

Thinking About Stars!

Science Texts

Directions: Choose at least two of these activities to complete.

Radical Reading

Reread "Classifying Stars." Highlight the words you think would be good in a glossary. Then, create a glossary for this piece of text. Write the words you highlighted in alphabetical order and add definitions.

Fun Fluency

Practice reading the poem fluently with a partner. When the two of you can recite it flawlessly, add some fun hand motions to go with the poem. You could also incorporate props. When you are ready, teach the poem and the hand motions to other students in another classroom or grade.

Wonderful Words

Stars are *shiny* and *sparkly*. They are *stunning* and *special*. How many adjectives that start with the letter *s* can you think of to describe stars? Make a list. Place a star next to your favorite word on the list!

Wacky Writing

Rewrite the poem from the star's point of view. How does the star view the human? What is the star thinking? Share your poem with a partner.

Atoms

Theme Summary

What do the air, a chair, and you all have in common? All of these things, including you, are made of atoms. Everything is made of atoms! In this pair of texts, students will explore the microscopically tiny world of atoms and molecules.

Standards

➡ Compare and contrast two or more characters, settings, or events in a story or drama, drawing on specific details in the text (e.g., how characters interact).

➡ Determine the meaning of general academic and domain-specific words and phrases in a text relevant to a grade 5 topic or subject area.

➡ Know that matter is made up of tiny particles called atoms, and different arrangements of atoms into groups compose all substances.

Materials

➡ *Elements, Molecules, and Mixtures* (page 75)

➡ *"Elements, Molecules, and Mixtures" Response* (page 76)

➡ *Adams and Mollycules* (pages 78–79)

➡ *"Adams and Mollycules" Response* (page 79)

➡ *Let's Compare! Here, There, and in the Square* (page 80)

➡ *Thinking About Atoms!* (page 81)

➡ pencils

➡ paper

Comparing the Texts

After students complete the lessons for each text, have them work in pairs or groups to reread both texts and complete the *Let's Compare! Here, There, and in the Square* activity page (page 80). Finally, students can work to complete the *Thinking About Atoms!* matrix (page 81). The matrix activities allow students to work on the important literacy skills of reading, writing, vocabulary, and fluency.

Answer Key

"Elements, Molecules, and Mixtures" Response (page 76)

1. B. tiny particles

2. Water is a compound because it is a molecule with *two or more atoms stuck together*. It is made from hydrogen and oxygen atoms (H_2O).

3. To separate a mixture, you use the *properties of the substances in the mixture*. You can use melting points, boiling points, magnets, or sieves.

"Adams and Mollycules" Response (page 79)

1. D. She thinks all are pretty cool.

2. Mom explains what water is made of in her last set of lines. She says *water is made of two hydrogen atoms and one oxygen atom*.

3. Molecules are formed when *atoms combine*.

Let's Compare! Here, There, and in the Square (page 80)

Students' information will vary. Check that the information in each column relates to one another.

Elements, Molecules, and Mixtures

Science Texts

	Lesson Steps	Teacher Think Alouds
Ready, Set, Predict!	• Provide the text to students and display a larger version. Have them do a quick and quiet text walk and pay attention to how the author chose to use headings. • Ask partners to predict the author's audience using the following: *I think the author wrote this for _____ (what audience) because _____.*	"Thinking about the author's audience helps me to better understand the text. Is the author writing this for scientists? Is the author writing this for students who love science? Is the author writing this for younger students who may not know a lot about science?"
Go! 	• Have students read the text independently to get an idea for what the text is about. • Direct students to circle the most challenging words they can find in the text.	"Challenging words for me are words that I do not understand, I do not know how to pronounce properly, or words that I think others will have difficulties with."
Reread to Clarify 	• Invite students to share their circled words with partners. Have partners work together to clarify their challenging words. • Have students look for additional words they find confusing. Work together as a class to clarify these words.	"I always confuse *microscope* and *telescope*. So, when I see the word *microscope* in the text I have to look it up in a dictionary to make sure I am thinking of the right word. Knowing the word makes the text easier to understand."
Reread to Question	• Place students into groups of three and have them reread the text to question. Provide each student with paper. One student writes a question about elements. Another student writes a question about molecules. The third student writes a question about mixtures. Students pass their papers to the right and answer the questions in front of them using evidence from the text. Then, pass the papers one more time so that all students in the groups have a chance to respond to the questions. • Have students respond to the question and prompts on page 76.	"My assigned word is *molecule*, so my question is 'How is a molecule made?' My group members might answer with *Atoms can join together to make molecules*."
Reread to Summarize and Respond	• Tell students to reread the text to summarize. Have them write a couple of sentences about each section of the text. Encourage students to use headings as they summarize.	

Elements, Molecules, and Mixtures

All matter is made of atoms, which are tiny particles. Even air is made of atoms. Atoms are extremely small. They are so small that a million billion of them can fit in a teaspoon. No one can see them without help, so it takes a strong microscope to see them.

Elements

When something is made of the same kind of atoms, it is called an element. It is very hard to turn one element into another element. In other words, iron will always be iron. You cannot turn it into other elements. You can heat it. You can hit it. You can drop it in acid. It does not matter what you do. It will still be iron. It might not look the same, but it will still be made of iron atoms.

Molecules

Atoms can join to make molecules. A molecule has two or more atoms stuck together. They become a new substance called a compound. The compound has different properties than the elements that make it.

For example, water is made from hydrogen and oxygen. But it is not like either of them. Water is a compound. Each water molecule has two kinds of atoms. This is written as H_2O. The number two means that there are two hydrogen atoms in the molecule. No number after the O means there is just one atom of oxygen.

Mixtures

A mixture is not the same as a compound. Some everyday mixtures are air and blood. They contain many different types of atoms and molecules. Not all of the atoms and molecules are joined through reactions. They can be separated easily if you know how.

The way to separate a mixture is to use the properties of the substances in the mixture. These properties are things such as the melting and boiling points. Another is whether it is magnetic. You can use magnets to separate out the magnetic molecules. And one more property is the size of its solid chunks. You can use a sieve to separate the big chunks from the small chunks.

Science Texts

"Elements, Molecules, and Mixtures" Response

Directions: Reread the text on page 75 to answer each question.

1. What are atoms?

    Ⓐ mixtures   Ⓒ compounds

    Ⓑ tiny particles   Ⓓ substances

2. Why is water a compound? Use phrases from the text in your answer.

_____

_____

_____

_____

_____

3. How do you separate a mixture? Use evidence from the text to support your answer.

_____

_____

_____

_____

_____

Fiction Text Teacher Notes

Adams and Mollycules

	Lesson Steps	Teacher Think Alouds
Ready, Set, Predict!	• Distribute the text to students and display a larger version. Ask students to notice how the text is organized. Ask them to predict what the text is about. • Discuss why the author organized the text into a reader's theater.	"I notice that the text is written like characters are talking to each other. The names of the characters are on the left. The words they say are on the right. Knowing how the text is organized will make it easier to read."
Go!	• Have students read the text independently and silently to begin to understand the content and to circle science-related words. • Allow students to share the words they circled. • Divide the class into four groups. Assign each group one role. Then, read the script chorally as a class.	
Reread to Clarify	• Tell groups to reread the text to clarify. Ask them to place asterisks (*) next to words they find tricky and would like to clarify. • Ask groups to use two or more different strategies to clarify the tricky words. Have them share the strategies they used to clarify their words with the class.	
Reread to Question	• Provide paper to the same groups. Tell them to fold the paper into fourths, labeling each section with one of the characters' names. • Ask groups to reread the text to question. Have them write questions about all of the characters that can be answered in the text. • Have students respond to the question and prompts on page 79.	"When thinking about Adam, I might ask 'What kind of characteristics does Adam have?' My group members might say he is excited because most of his lines end in exclamation marks."
Reread to Summarize and Respond	• Tell students to reread the text to summarize. Have them write reviews that highlight the main ideas of the text. • Ask volunteers to share their summaries with the class.	"As I begin to write my review, I want to make sure that I highlight the main idea and key details in the text. Then, I want to include whether I like each part or not and why."

*Note: For more tips, engagement strategies, and fluency options to include in this lesson, see pages 122–128.

Adams and Mollycules

Adam: Hey, look, Mom, I'm an atom!

Mom: (*noticing Adam's flashy superhero outfit*) Uh, well, honey, you're something all right. But what exactly do you think an atom is?

Adam: It's a supercharged superhero, like me!

Mom: Well, I'll admit, the cape is a nice touch, but I think maybe you're a little confused.

Neutron: Arf!

Mom: That's enough from you, Neutron.

Molly: Seriously. And besides, it's not "Adam," it's "atom." And molecules are cooler anyway.

Adam: It's not "Molly-cules," you know!

Molly: Well, it should be.

Neutron: Arf!

Mom: Okay, okay, enough! Adam and Molly-cule are both pretty cool.

Neutron: Arf!

Mom: And yes, you, too, Neutron. But let's take a look at what *atoms* and *molecules* really are, okay?

Molly and Adam: Okay.

Mom: Atoms are pretty super, just like you guys. But they are super tiny—much smaller than you can see without a microscope. Everything everywhere is made of atoms.

Adam: See, they're so super they make up everything!

Molly: Well, what about molecules, Mom?

Mom: Atoms combine to form molecules. There are different types of atoms, and they can combine in different amounts.

Neutron: Arf!

Adams and Mollycules (cont.)

Mom: Enough, Neutron. So molecules are super, too. When they are made of all the same type of atom, they are called elements, such as hydrogen or oxygen. When they are made of different types of atoms, they are called compounds, such as water. Water is made of two hydrogen atoms and one oxygen atom. Together, the atoms make water molecules.

Adam: Hey, Molly, want to play superhero atoms and molecules with me?

Molly: Sure. After all, Molly-cules need Adams, don't they?

Neutron: I could have told you that!

• •

"Adams and Mollycules" Response

Directions: Reread the script on pages 78–79 to answer each question.

1. Which one does the mom think is cooler: atoms, elements, or molecules?

   Ⓐ atoms   ⓒ elements

   Ⓑ molecules   Ⓓ She thinks all are pretty cool.

2. What is water made of? Where in the text can you find the answer?

   _____

   _____

   _____

3. How are molecules formed? Use evidence from the text to support your answer.

   _____

   _____

   _____

Let's Compare!

Here, There, and in the Square

Directions: Reread both texts. Find two separate pieces of information that appear in both texts. Write the information as it appears in each text on the lines. Then, illustrate that information.

Information Set #1	Information Set #2
From "Adams and Mollycules":	From "Adams and Mollycules":
_____	_____
_____	_____
_____	_____
_____	_____
_____	_____
From "Elements, Molecules, and Mixtures":	From "Elements, Molecules, and Mixtures":
_____	_____
_____	_____
_____	_____
_____	_____
_____	_____
Illustration:	Illustration:

Science Texts

Name:_____ Date:_____

Thinking About Atoms!

Directions: Choose at least two of these activities to complete.

Radical Reading

Reread "Elements, Molecules, and Mixtures." Use a red marker to underline your favorite fact. Use a blue marker to underline a topic you want to learn more about.

Fun Fluency

Practice reading the "Adams and Mollycules" reader's theater script with some classmates. When all of you can read it fluently, perform it for younger classes or record it as a radio performance.

Wonderful Words

Imagine you have to travel to another galaxy and explain what atoms and molecules are to the aliens there. Make a list of all the words you would want them to know. Then, create your own alien language and rewrite your list of words in that language.

Wacky Writing

Use the information from "Elements, Molecules, and Mixtures" to write another scene for the "Adams and Mollycules" reader's theater script. Share your scene with a partner.

Unit 9 Overview
Cells

Theme Summary

You can't see them with the naked eye but they are a part of every single living thing. These building blocks of life are called cells! In this pair of texts, a clever and creative poem on these small units of life is paired with a nonfiction piece on the importance of cells.

Answer Key

"The Building Blocks of Life" Response (page 85)

1. C. Rudolf Virchow

2. Cells use food to make energy, which people then use to move, eat, and sleep.

3. Chlorophyll is important because it absorbs energy from the sun and uses it to make food. This is called *photosynthesis*. As a result, it releases oxygen into the air. We could not survive without oxygen.

"Microscopic Wonders" Response (page 88)

1. A. microscope

2. The author uses the simile *looking like a jellied goo* to describe the cell she sees.

3. The author lists *stem*, *limb*, *tail*, and *wing* as living things in the last stanza.

Let's Compare! Making More Cells Stanzas (page 89)

Students' additional stanzas will vary. Check that the stanzas make sense and reflect information about cells.

Standards

➡ Describe how a narrator's or speaker's point of view influences how events are described.

➡ Draw on information from multiple print or digital sources, demonstrating the ability to locate an answer to a question quickly or to solve a problem efficiently.

➡ Know that cells convert energy obtained from food to carry on the many functions needed to sustain life.

Materials

➡ *The Building Blocks of Life* (pages 84–85)

➡ *"The Building Blocks of Life" Response* (page 85)

➡ *Microscopic Wonders* (page 87)

➡ *"Microscopic Wonders" Response* (page 88)

➡ *Let's Compare! Making More Cells Stanzas* (page 89)

➡ *Thinking About Cells!* (page 90)

➡ pencils

➡ highlighters

➡ Internet

Comparing the Texts

After students complete the lessons for each text, have them work in pairs or groups to reread both texts and complete the *Let's Compare! Making More Cells Stanzas* activity page (page 89). Finally, students can work to complete the *Thinking About Cells!* matrix (page 90). The matrix activities allow students to work on the important literacy skills of reading, writing, vocabulary, and fluency.

The Building Blocks of Life

	Lesson Steps	Teacher Think Alouds
Ready, Set, Predict!	• Distribute the text to students and display a larger version. Have students skim the subtitles and picture captions. • Engage the class in a discussion using the following prompt: *I think the author will use high-level scientific vocabulary in this text because _____.*	"I scan a page before I begin to read. I look for text features such as subtitles, charts, images, or captions that will help me to better understand the text I am about to read. I see pictures of cells, so perhaps this text is about cells."
Go!	• Have students read the text independently. Ask them to circle any words they do not understand or find confusing. • Read the text aloud as students follow along. Have them cross out any words they circled if they now understand the word after the second reading.	
Reread to Clarify	• Tell students to reread the text in pairs to clarify it. Ask pairs to discuss any words they still have circled using the following: *The word _____ is tricky, so I _____.* • Invite pairs to discuss with other pairs the strategies they used to clarify the words they circled.	"The word *photosynthesis* is tricky, so I look up the word in the dictionary. I learn that it is a process that takes place when a plant is exposed to sunlight."
Reread to Question	• Have students reread the text in pairs to question. Have partners take turns asking questions about the main text. • Ask them to highlight where in the text they find the answers to one anothers' questions. You may wish to have them search the Internet for more support to the answers. • Have students respond to the question and prompts on page 85.	
Reread to Summarize and Respond	• Invite pairs to reread the text to summarize. Tell them to identify the most important points and to put the points in their own words. Invite students to act out their favorite facts. • Ask pairs what additional information they would include if they were the authors.	"Before I begin to verbally summarize the text to my partner, I will reread the text and place asterisks (*) next to the important parts."

*Note: For more tips, engagement strategies, and fluency options to include in this lesson, see pages 122–128.

The Building Blocks of Life

Science Texts

Have you ever seen a cell? Cells are the smallest units of life. They are called the building blocks of life. We cannot see individual cells with our naked eyes. We must use a microscope to see them.

The importance of cells is outlined in Cell Theory. Three scientists were working on cells at about the same time. Their names were Matthias Schleiden, Theodor Schwann, and Rudolf Virchow. Together, their work became known as Cell Theory.

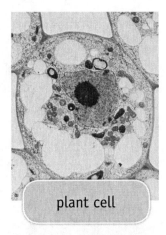

plant cell

Schleiden worked with plant cells, and Schwann worked with animal cells. One night, they had dinner together. They talked about their work. They realized that the cells they both studied were very similar. Plants and animals were both made of cells.

They went to the laboratory and looked at cells. Then they published their findings in 1839. They said two important things. First, all living things are made of cells. Second, cells are the smallest part of a living thing that is itself alive.

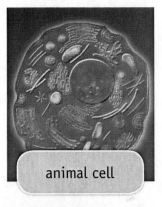

animal cell

The one thing that they were not sure of was where cells came from. Almost 20 years later, Rudolf Virchow solved the puzzle. Cells, he said, come from other cells. This became the third part of Cell Theory.

Cells are filled with fluid that is like gelatin. The fluid is called cytoplasm. It is made of cytosol. Cytosol is like a special soup that has everything the cell needs to live.

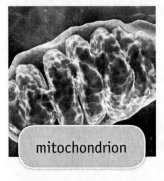

mitochondrion

A cell must do many different jobs to survive. Inside the fluid, there are many different cell parts called organelles. Each organelle does a different job. Some organelles turn food into energy. Other organelles store water. Most organelles are separated from the cytosol by a membrane. The membrane is like a skin that only lets in what the organelle needs. Everything else is kept outside.

Where do we get the energy we need to move, eat, and sleep? It comes from cells. Mitochondria are organelles that change food into energy cells can use. This is called cellular respiration. Cellular respiration needs oxygen. Mitochondria break apart molecules of food and release the energy. Then the cell uses the energy to build new proteins, move molecules around the cell, and make more cells.

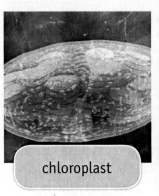

chloroplast

The Building Blocks of Life (cont.)

Science Texts

Both plant and animal cells have mitochondria. Plant cells have chloroplasts, too. These are organelles that use energy from light. Chloroplasts contain a pigment. It is called chlorophyll. Chlorophyll absorbs energy from the sun or other sources of light. The chloroplast uses that energy to make food from water and carbon dioxide. This process of making food is called photosynthesis. As a result of this process, oxygen is released into the air. We need oxygen to survive!

"The Building Blocks of Life" Response

Directions: Reread the text on pages 84–85 to answer each question.

1. Which scientist figured out where cells come from?

    Ⓐ Matthias Schleiden   Ⓒ Rudolf Virchow

    Ⓑ Theodor Schwann   Ⓓ Albert Einstein

2. How are cells related to humans moving, eating, and sleeping?

    _____

    _____

    _____

    _____

    _____

3. Why is chlorophyll important? Use evidence from the text to support your answer.

    _____

    _____

    _____

    _____

    _____

Fiction Text Teacher Notes

Microscopic Wonders

	Lesson Steps	Teacher Think Alouds
Ready, Set, Predict!	• Read the title aloud to students. Ask them what *microscopic* means. Give partners a few minutes to discuss everything they can think of that is microscopic. Write student responses on the board. • Distribute the text to students and display a larger version.	"I know that *microscopic* means 'small,' so I think this text will be about small things."
Go!	• Have students read the poem independently and silently. Ask them to circle all the synonyms they find for the word *small*. • Read the poem aloud as students follow along. Model fluent reading and tone.	"When I circle all of the synonyms for the word *small*, it helps me remember what the poem is about."
Reread to Clarify	• Instruct students to reread the text with partners to clarify. Have students switch back and forth with each verse. Ask students to underline any words they think first graders would have trouble understanding. Have the pairs use strategies to clarify the words for a first-grade student. • Invite students to share with the class the strategies they used to clarify the words using the following prompt: *The word _____ may be confusing for a first grader, so we _____.*	"The word *microscopic* may be confusing for first grade, so I would tell them it means something that is small and can only be seen with a microscope. Then, I would show them a picture of a microscope and tell them what it is and what things scientists look at through microscopes."
Reread to Question	• Direct partners to reread the text to question. Have the pairs take turns asking and answering questions about the text such as *How does the author of the poem feel about cells?* • Have students respond to the question and prompts on page 88.	
Reread to Summarize and Respond	• Ask partners to reread the text to summarize. Have them write each stanza in their own words. Invite students to add illustrations to their sentences. • Review the close reading strategies by singing the song on page 128.	

*Note:** For more tips, engagement strategies, and fluency options to include in this lesson, see pages 122–128.

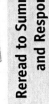

Microscopic Wonders

Itty bitty tiny cell,
I can't see you very well.
Well, the truth is not at all;
I'm too big and you're too small.

Microscopic is your size.
I can't see you with my eyes,
'Less I use a microscope.
Which in truth's my only hope.

Through the lens you seem to grow;
Finally I say, "Hello,
How's it goin', little cell?
Hey, you're looking very well."

Just a squirmy little mass,
Nucleus and protoplast,
Looking like a jellied goo,
Hard to see what you can do.

But I know you are the trade
Out of which all life is made—
Smallest bit that is alive,
Out of which we all can thrive.

Wonder all the cells I own
From eye to ear, blood to bone;
Wonder all the things they do!
How can I be made of you?

But you are the tiny crumbs,
Stuff and fluff from which life comes.
Cells dividing, and again,
Making more new cells and then

Part of every living thing,
Stem and limb and tail and wing.
Living things—a cell parade,
Specks from which we all are made.

Science Texts

"Microscopic Wonders" Response

Directions: Reread the poem on page 87 to answer each question.

1. What tool do you need to use to see a cell?

    Ⓐ microscope   Ⓒ the naked eye

    Ⓑ protoplast   Ⓓ telescope

2. What simile does the author use to describe the cell she sees?

_____

_____

_____

_____

_____

3. What examples of living things does the author include in the last stanza?

_____

_____

_____

_____

_____

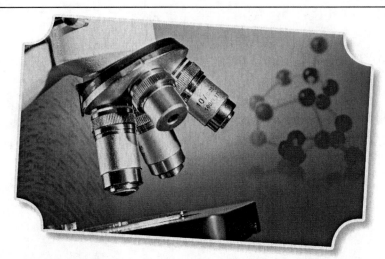

Name:_____ Date:_____

Making More Cells Stanzas

Directions: Reread both texts. Remember that cells come from other cells. Use the additional information in the nonfiction text on cells to make more stanzas for the "Microscopic Wonders" poem. You can add stanzas to the beginning, middle, or end of the poem. Use the word bank below to help get the creative juices flowing!

Word Bank				
Cell Theory	plant cells	chlorophyll	animal cells	organelles
food	energy	mitochondria	photosynthesis	

_____

_____

_____

_____

_____

_____

_____

_____

_____

_____

_____

_____

_____

_____

_____

_____

Thinking About Cells!

Directions: Choose at least two of these activities to complete.

Radical Reading

Sometimes illustrations can help a reader understand confusing text or a tricky subject. Reread "The Building Blocks of Life" and think of any additional illustrations that may help make the text easier to understand. Draw these illustrations on a sheet of paper. Share them with a classmate. Ask the student if the drawings help to clarify the text.

Fun Fluency

Practice reading "Microscopic Wonders." Pay close attention to the punctuation used in the poem. Make sure your tone and voice reflect question marks, exclamation marks, and quotations. When you feel comfortable, recite the poem for your friends.

Wonderful Words

Let's tap into Greek roots! *Micro* means "extremely small" and *scope* means "to see." Think of other words that contain these roots and create definitions for those words. Share your words and definitions with a partner.

Wacky Writing

Imagine you could send a letter back in time to Rudolf Virchow. What questions would you ask him about cells? What would you tell him about scientific research today? Write an inquisitive and informative letter to Mr. Virchow.

American Indians and Westward Expansion

Theme Summary

America's past is not without tragedy. In this unit, students will learn about the heartbreaking plight of the American Indians during America's westward expansion. Students will read a poem about an American Indian who wants to return home to his land in the far west and an emotional surrender speech by Chief Joseph.

Standards

➡ Explain how a series of chapters, scenes, or stanzas fits together to provide the overall structure of a particular story, drama, or poem.

➡ Quote accurately from a text when explaining what the text says explicitly and when drawing inferences from the text.

➡ Understand significant events for Native American tribes in the late 19th century and how they responded.

Materials

➡ *I Will Fight No More Forever* (page 93)

➡ *"I Will Fight No More Forever" Response* (page 94)

➡ *The Indian's Prayer* (page 96)

➡ *"The Indian's Prayer" Response* (page 97)

➡ *Let's Compare! Flip and Switch* (page 98)

➡ *Thinking About American Indians!* (page 99)

➡ pencils

➡ scissors

Comparing the Texts

After students complete the lessons for each text, have them work in pairs or groups to reread both texts and complete the *Let's Compare! Flip and Switch* activity page (page 98). Finally, students can work to complete the *Thinking About American Indians!* matrix (page 99). The matrix activities allow students to work on the important literacy skills of reading, writing, vocabulary, and fluency.

Answer Key

"I Will Fight No More Forever" Response (page 94)

1. D. Chief Joseph

2. Chief Joseph is *tired of fighting*. He has lost too many of his own men to death (including Looking Glass and Ta Hool Hool Shute). His heart is *sick and sad*.

3. Chief Joseph cares for his people very much. He is worried about them *freezing to death*. He worries that they have *no blankets, no food*. He wants to go find them. He promises he will *fight no more forever* so he can go and find his people.

"The Indian's Prayer" Response (page 97)

1. C. his mother's heart

2. His home is in the *far distant west*. It is in the *woods* or *wild forest* as there are *tall cedars* and a *cataract* along with *groves of the glen*.

3. He wants to go see the cataract where he spent his younger days and see his mother and father.

Let's Compare! Flip and Switch (page 98)

Students' poems or speeches will vary. Check that the format has been flipped. For the second activity, the similarity is that both texts discuss wanting the fighting to stop. In "I Will Fight No More Forever," the lines *I am tired of fighting* and *From where the sun now stands, I will fight no more forever* support this. In "The Indian's Prayer," the repeated line *let me go* supports this.

Nonfiction Text Teacher Notes
I Will Fight No More Forever

	Lesson Steps	**Teacher Think Alouds**
Ready, Set, Predict!	• Distribute the text to students and display a larger version. Read the title, the author's name, and the year aloud. Ask students if they know what was happening to American Indians during the 1800s in the United States. • Have them list prior knowledge they have of American Indian history.	"I think about everything I already know about American Indians and the events that shaped their history. Any information I already know will help me better understand the text."
Go!	• Have students read the text independently. Tell them to place asterisks (*) next to words or phrases that they found interesting. • Reread the text aloud for students. Model fluent reading. Tell students to pay attention to your tone, where you pause, and how you pronounce words.	"I notice that there is not a lot of text in this piece. However, there is a lot of information. I will make sure to read slowly and clearly. This makes the text easier to understand."
Reread to Clarify	• Ask students to reread the text independently to clarify. Ask them to underline sentences that they had to read twice to understand. • Tell students to work in small groups to help one another clarify the parts of the text they underlined. Invite them to share with one another the strategies they use (e.g., *rereading, reading on, visualizing*).	
Reread to Question	• Instruct small groups to reread the text to formulate questions. Have each group write one question that can be answered by quoting a line from the text. • Direct the groups to pass their questions clockwise so that another group can find the quote that answers the question. • Have students respond to the question and prompts on page 94.	
Reread to Summarize and Respond	• Place students in pairs. Have pairs reread the text to summarize. Tell them to write Chief Joseph's speech in their own words. • Ask student volunteers to share their summaries with the class.	"I am going to imagine that I am Chief Joseph making this speech. I might start by saying that I do not want to fight anymore."

*Note: For more tips, engagement strategies, and fluency options to include in this lesson, see pages 122–128.

I Will Fight No More Forever

Social Studies Texts

by Chief Joseph of the Nez Perce, 1877

Tell General Howard I know his heart. What he told me before, I have it in my heart. I am tired of fighting. Our Chiefs are killed; Looking Glass is dead, Ta Hool Hool Shute is dead. The old men are all dead. It is the young men who say yes or no. He who led on the young men is dead. It is cold, and we have no blankets; the little children are freezing to death. My people, some of them, have run away to the hills, and have no blankets, no food. No one knows where they are—perhaps freezing to death. I want to have time to look for my children, and see how many of them I can find. Maybe I shall find them among the dead. Hear me, my Chiefs! I am tired; my heart is sick and sad. From where the sun now stands I will fight no more forever.

Social Studies Texts

"I Will Fight No More Forever" Response

Directions: Reread the text on page 93 to answer each question.

1. Who is delivering this speech?

   Ⓐ General Howard   Ⓒ a young American Indian man

   Ⓑ Looking Glass   Ⓓ Chief Joseph

2. Why is Chief Joseph surrendering? What details in the text support your answer?

_____

_____

_____

_____

_____

_____

_____

3. How would you describe Chief Joseph's relationship with his people? Use evidence from the text to support your answer.

_____

_____

_____

_____

_____

_____

Fiction Text Teacher Notes
The Indian's Prayer

	Lesson Steps	Teacher Think Alouds
Ready, Set, Predict!	• Read the title of the text aloud to students. Have students turn to partners and predict what the text will be about using the following: *I think this text is about _____ because _____.* • Distribute the text to students and display a larger version.	"The title of a text sometimes tells the main idea or at least gives clues as to what the text is about. I read the title 'The Indian's Prayer.' As I read the text, I will look to see which sentences in the text include details about what the Indian is praying for."
Go!	• Tell students to read the poem independently and silently. Ask them to circle any phrases that repeat in the poem. • Read the poem aloud as students follow along. Model fluent reading. Ask students why the poet repeats certain lines.	"The poet may be repeating lines to emphasize important parts of the text. As I read, I will pay close attention to these parts."
Reread to Clarify	• Have students reread the poem in pairs to clarify. Have them underline phrases that help them visualize and clarify the meaning of the poem and discuss the phrase using the following: *When I read the phrase _____, I visualize _____.* • Invite students to transfer the images they visualized in their heads to paper to help further clarify the poem.	"When I read the phrase *where the tall cedars wave and the bright waters flow*, I visualize big, green bushy Christmasy-like trees with a clean, cold, and crisp river flowing through the trees. It is a beautiful scene, and perhaps its beauty is one of the reasons the Indian wants to return."
Reread to Question	• Instruct students to reread the poem in small groups to question. Pose these questions to students: *What structure does the poem have? How do the stanzas fit together?* • Invite students to generate questions to go with each stanza. Tell groups to meet with other groups to answer their questions. • Have students respond to the question and prompts on page 97.	
Reread to Summarize and Respond	• Ask students to reread the text to summarize. Have them cut the stanzas apart and shuffle them. Have them work in their groups to place the stanzas back in order. Guide students to discuss how the author speaks of childhood, boyhood, adulthood (in battle), and then concludes with a reference to his ashes.	"I think the stanza with the line *To the scenes of my childhood in innocence blest* should be first because the poem goes from the earlier years to ashes."

*Note: For more tips, engagement strategies, and fluency options to include in this lesson, see pages 122–128.

The Indian's Prayer

by Anonymous, 1846

Let me go to my home in the far distant west,

To the scenes of my childhood in innocence blest;
Where the tall cedars wave and the bright waters flow,
Where my fathers repose. Let me go, let me go.
Where my fathers repose. Let me go, let me go.

Let me go to the spot where the cataract plays,
Where oft I have sported in boyhood's bright days,
And greet my poor mother, whose heart will o'erflow
At the sight of the child, let me go, let me go.

At the sight of the child, let me go, let me go.

Let me go to my sire, by whose battlescar'd side,
I have sported so oft in the morn of my pride,
And exulted to conquer the insolent foe,

To my father, the chief, let me go, let me go.
To my father, the chief, let me go, let me go.

And oh! Let me go to my wild forest home

No more from it life-cheering pleasures to roam.
'Neath the groves of the glen, let my ashes lie low
To my home in the woods, let me go, let me go.
To my home in the woods, let me go, let me go.

"The Indian's Prayer" Response

Directions: Reread the poem on page 96 to answer each question.

1. Whose heart will overflow upon seeing the speaker of the poem?

   Ⓐ his chief's heart   Ⓒ his mother's heart

   Ⓑ his sire's heart   Ⓓ his father's heart

2. Where is the poet's home? What text evidence supports your answer?

   _____

   _____

   _____

   _____

   _____

   _____

   _____

3. What does the poet want to do when he returns home? How do you know?

   _____

   _____

   _____

   _____

   _____

   _____

Social Studies Texts

Let's Compare!

Flip and Switch

Directions: Reread both texts. Both are powerful and moving. Each one makes an important statement in its original format. Will they remain just as potent and touching if the formats are flipped? Challenge yourself to write Chief Joseph's speech as a poem, or write "The Indian's Prayer" as a brief speech made by the speaker. Write the final draft of your poem or speech on the lines below.

_____

_____

_____

_____

_____

_____

_____

_____

_____

_____

_____

_____

_____

• •

Directions: Write a few sentences in which you note the similarities between these two texts. Use evidence from each text to support your point.

_____

_____

_____

_____

Name:_____ Date:_____

Thinking About American Indians!

Directions: Choose at least two of these activities to complete.

Radical Reading

Reread "The Indian's Prayer." Highlight the last six words in each stanza. Why do you think the poet repeats these words over and over again? Write a few sentences explaining your thoughts on this technique.

Fun Fluency

Practice reading "The Indian's Prayer" in different tones. Try a serious tone, an angry tone, and then with sadness in your voice. Which tone is the most appropriate for this poem? After you have decided and can recite the poem fluently, perform your version for family and friends.

Wonderful Words

Reread "I Will Fight No More Forever." What is Chief Joseph feeling? Make a list of 10 adjectives that describe how you think Chief Joseph felt at the time he gave this speech.

Wacky Writing

Imagine you are a reporter for a newspaper in 1877. You are witnessing Chief Joseph give his surrender speech. How would you describe his speech to others? What would you say about it? Write a newspaper column covering that day's events regarding Chief Joseph.

Unit 11 Overview
Lewis and Clark

Theme Summary

It is an adventure story for the ages, a daring journey through uncharted lands during America's westward expansion. In May 1804, the Lewis and Clark expedition began! Students will read a reader's theater script about one of the most important members of the corps and a nonfiction text that briefly summarizes the long momentous tale of persistence and courage.

Answer Key

"The Westward Journey of Lewis and Clark" Response (page 103)

1. A. St. Louis, Missouri

2. They kept journals that described the weather, made maps, and illustrated the new plants and animals they saw.

3. Answers may include: They saw bison, coyotes, prairie dogs. They travelled through North Dakota, down the Missouri River, over the Rocky Mountains, down the Snake River, into Oregon and to the Pacific Ocean. They met Mandan Indians, a fur trapper named Toussaint Charbonneau, Sacagawea, and Shoshone tribes.

"Sacagawea Saves the Day" Response (page 106)

1. D. She is telling the Shoshone she is one of them.

2. Great Spirit is a mother-nature type figure that the American Indians greatly respect and turn to for guidance. Sacagawea thanks Great Spirit for leading her to her tribe. Great Spirit wants everyone to *live in harmony together*.

3. Cameahwait is *disappointed* when Clark is late and feels this may be a warning that they should not trust the white men. Cameahwait's feelings change when he learns that Sacagawea of the Shoshone tribe is also his sister.

Let's Compare! Journaling History (page 107)

Student's journal entries will vary. Check that facts included are from the text pair.

Standards

➡ Compare and contrast two or more characters, settings, or events in a story or drama, drawing on specific details in the text (e.g., how characters interact).

➡ Explain the relationships or interactions between two or more individuals, events, ideas, or concepts in a historical, scientific, or technical text based on specific information in the text.

➡ Know about expeditions of American explorers.

Materials

➡ *The Westward Journey of Lewis and Clark* (pages 102–103)

➡ *"The Westward Journey of Lewis and Clark" Response* (page 103)

➡ *Sacagawea Saves the Day* (pages 105–106)

➡ *"Sacagawea Saves the Day" Response* (page 106)

➡ *Let's Compare! Journaling History* (page 107)

➡ *Thinking About Lewis and Clark!* (page 108)

➡ highlighters

➡ pencils

Comparing the Texts

After students complete the lessons for each text, have them work in pairs or groups to reread both texts and complete the *Let's Compare! Journaling History* activity page (page 107). Finally, students can work to complete the *Thinking About Lewis and Clark!* matrix (page 108). The matrix activities allow students to work on the important literacy skills of reading, writing, vocabulary, and fluency.

Nonfiction Text Teacher Notes

The Westward Journey of Lewis and Clark

	Lesson Steps	Teacher Think Alouds
Ready, Set, Predict!	• Read the title and first sentence of the text aloud to the class. Ask students to predict the author's purpose for writing this text using the following prompt: *I think the author wrote this to _____ because _____.* • Distribute the text to students and display a larger version.	"Before I read a text, I think about the author's purpose. Did the author write the text to entertain me, to persuade me, or maybe to inform me about a topic? Understanding the author's purpose helps me better understand the text."
Go!	• Have students read the text independently and silently. Ask them to highlight text that supports their predictions and underline text that proves their predictions may be incorrect. Discuss whether their predictions were correct. • Read the text aloud. Model fluent reading.	
Reread to Clarify	• Tell students to reread the text independently to clarify. Have them place stars next to any parts they had to read twice in order to see clear pictures in their heads. • Invite students to pair-share the parts of the text they placed stars by. Then, have students illustrate their partners' starred texts to help clarify the text.	"I have to reread the third paragraph to visualize it. My visualization does not match my partner's drawing because the drawing shows the path going around the mountains instead of through them. By telling my partner this, we have a better understanding of the text."
Reread to Question	• Instruct students to remain in their pairs and reread the text to question. Ask them to highlight any information that explains the relationship between Lewis and Clark and the American Indians. Invite students to ask questions to each other such as: *What kind of relationship did these two groups of people have?* • Have students respond to the question and prompts on page 103.	"When I reread the text to question, I make sure that the answers can be found in the text. For example, my question is 'What is the purpose of the expedition?' My partner can highlight the phrase *to explore this new land.*"
Reread to Summarize and Respond	• Ask students to reread the text to summarize. Tell them to create annotated timelines of the events. • Invite students to add illustrations to their timelines.	

*****Note:** For more tips, engagement strategies, and fluency options to include in this lesson, see pages 122–128.

The Westward Journey of Lewis and Clark

President Thomas Jefferson wanted to know all about the Louisiana Territory, so he decided to send a group of men on an expedition to explore this new land. Jefferson appointed Meriwether Lewis the leader of the expedition. Lewis chose the rest of his crew after first asking William Clark, an old army friend, to be his co-captain.

Lewis traveled to St. Louis, Missouri, in the winter of 1803–1804. There, he met his crew of about 40 men called the Corps of Discovery. The men set up camp and spent months training. They built boats, exercised, and practiced shooting.

The Corps of Discovery began its journey on May 14, 1804. They planned to travel northwest along the Missouri River. This would lead them to the Rocky Mountains. There, they would cross a pass through the mountains. Rivers on the other side would take them to the Pacific Ocean.

Both captains kept journals in which they wrote about their adventures. They carefully recorded the weather and made maps of the land and the water. They described and illustrated all of the new plants and animals that they saw, including bison, coyotes, prairie dogs, and jackrabbits.

By November 1804, the crew reached what is now North Dakota. They befriended the Mandan Indians and decided to stay in one of their villages until spring. They built a camp called Fort Mandan. That winter the crew hired a new member named Toussaint Charbonneau. He was a fur trapper who lived with the Mandan people. His young Shoshone Indian wife, Sacagawea, had just given birth to a baby boy. They joined the expedition.

The Westward Journey of Lewis and Clark (cont)

In April 1805, the team set off again on the Missouri River. They started across the Rocky Mountain pass in September. The men had never seen such big mountains and had not realized how long the crossing would take. At last, the group made it to the other side of the Rockies. They built five new canoes, and they went down the Snake River into the area of land called Oregon. There, the river flowed into the Columbia River, which flowed into the Pacific Ocean.

On November 7, 1805, the group was overjoyed when it saw the Pacific Ocean in the distance.

• •

"The Westward Journey of Lewis and Clark" Response

Directions: Reread the text on pages 102–103 to answer each question.

1. Where did Lewis and Clark train their men for the journey?

   Ⓐ St. Louis, Missouri　　　　Ⓒ North Dakota

   Ⓑ the Rocky Mountains　　　Ⓓ Washington, D.C.

2. How do we know so much about Lewis and Clark's journey today?

   _____

   _____

   _____

3. Use the text to list some of the places, people, and things Lewis and Clark saw on their journey.

   _____

   _____

   _____

   _____

Fiction Text Teacher Notes
Sacagawea Saves the Day

	Lesson Steps	Teacher Think Alouds
Ready, Set, Predict!	• Distribute the text and display a larger version. Ask students what they notice about the format of the text. • Discuss the format of the reader's theater. Ask students to discuss the following: *I think the author wrote the text in a reader's theater format because _____.*	"When I look at how the text is organized, I can see that it is written in a script form. This helps me understand that characters will talk to one another."
Go!	• Have students read the text silently and underline proper nouns they find interesting. Ask partners to share their proper nouns. • Divide the class into five groups. Assign each group a role in the script. Then, choral read the script as a class.	"When I read my part, I will pay close attention to punctuation, such as question marks and exclamation marks, so that I read it fluently."
Reread to Clarify	• Tell groups to reread the text to clarify. Ask them to circle parts they find confusing. • Ask groups to share with the class the confusing parts they selected. Have the class work together to clarify some of the parts that most students circled (e.g., *read on, ask a friend*).	
Reread to Question	• Tell groups to reread the text to question. Ask them to select two characters they find interesting and underline sentences and words that go with the selected characters. • Invite students to compare and contrast the two characters. Then, ask each group to write one question about each character that can be answered using evidence from the text. Answer the questions as a class. • Have students respond to the question and prompts on page 106.	"Comparing and contrasting the characters in a text helps me better understand the characters themselves and the text as a whole. For example, I might compare Scout and Lewis. In the beginning of the script, Scout is cautious while Lewis is confident."
Reread to Summarize and Respond	• Tell students to reread the script to summarize. Ask them to state the role each character played in the plot. • Ask students to select their favorite characters and draw sketches of them.	

*Note: For more tips, engagement strategies, and fluency options to include in this lesson, see pages 122–128.

Sacagawea Saves the Day

by Kathleen E. Bradley

Cameahwait: You said that the rest of your party would be here soon and would be ready to barter. We are extremely disappointed.

Scout: We delayed our bison hunt by three days and have walked many miles away from the hunt. Everyone believes we are being led into a trap. We should have never trusted these white men.

Lewis: I tell you our people are coming. I'm sure they are late because the river is so treacherous.

Scout: Chief Cameahwait, maybe it is Great Spirit's feeling that this land is not for white men.

Lewis: Look west! Captain Clark and the rest of the party have finally arrived!

Clark: Oh! Captain Lewis, ol' friend! It sure is good to see you again!

Lewis: Captain Clark, what is Sacagawea doing? Why is she dancing with her fingertips to her mouth?

Scout: Through this dance she is telling us that she is of our nation. This is why my people are all shouting and rejoicing! They are happy.

Sacagawea: He is right! They speak my language, and I recognize their dress and ways. We have finally found the Shoshone! Thank you, Great Spirit!

Lewis: Chief Cameahwait, you can now see, we are men of our words. Our party has arrived as promised. We have our goods here and are ready to barter.

Sacagawea: The chief has laid down a white cloth for us to sit upon. It means he is ready to negotiate.

Clark: We, too, promise to barter fairly. The Shoshone people are known for their excellent horses.

Cameahwait: I raise this sacred pipe first to the heavens. Then, I raise it in every direction that the wind blows across Great Spirit's land. We will each draw smoke from it to show our unity. It is Great Spirit's way that all who walk this earth live in harmony together.

Sacagawea: Chief, what is it about you that seems so familiar to me?

Name:_____ Date: _____

Sacagawea Saves the Day (cont)

Clark: Sacagawea, your eyes are filling with tears. What's wrong?

Sacagawea: Oh, nothing is wrong! Everything is absolutely perfect! These are not tears of sadness, but tears of pure joy. Chief, do you not recognize me? I am your sister! Our appearances have changed so much since we last met. Five summers ago, you were but a boy, and I was just a young girl.

Cameahwait: Sister, it is you! I have hoped for a day such as this for so long.

Scout: I doubted these men, but now I believe Great Spirit has led them to us.

Sacagawea: Captains, Great Spirit did not lead you to just any tribe—he led you to my tribe! Brother, know that these men are honorable. Great Spirit guides them.

"Sacagawea Saves the Day" Response

Directions: Reread the script on pages 105–106 to answer each question.

1. Why does Sacagawea dance?

   Ⓐ She is happy.

   Ⓑ She is warning Lewis and Clark.

   Ⓒ She is thanking Great Spirit.

   Ⓓ She is telling the Shoshone she is one of them.

2. Who is Great Spirit? Use evidence from the text to support your answer.

   _____

   _____

   _____

3. How do Cameahwait's feelings change toward Lewis and Clark?

   _____

   _____

   _____

Let's Compare!

Journaling History

Directions: Reread both texts. Use the texts to write at least five facts in the journal about the Lewis and Clark expedition. Include drawings, too!

Thinking About Lewis and Clark!

Directions: Choose at least two of these activities to complete.

Radical Reading

Reread the excerpt "The Westward Journey of Lewis and Clark." Place a star next to two parts of the text you want to know more about. Then, do some research about the journey and add a few new sentences to the text.

Fun Fluency

Practice reading "Sacagawea Saves the Day" with a group of friends. Be sure you are pronouncing the character's names correctly. Remember to speak clearly and reflect the punctuation in your voice. When you and your group are ready, perform the script for your class.

Wonderful Words

A synonym is a word that means the same or almost the same thing as another word. Make a list of all the synonyms you can think of for the word *journey*.

Wacky Writing

Write a detailed journal entry about a time you did something new and adventurous. Include sketches in your journal.

The Civil War

Theme Summary

From 1861 to 1865 America was divided and embattled in one of the bloodiest periods in its history. The outcome of the Civil War would unite the country as one and bring about the end of slavery. In this unit, students will read about the Battle of Shiloh, a patriotic song from the nation's past, and read a nonfiction text about how our government works. **Note:** You may wish to have students research background information on the Battle of Shiloh prior to this unit.

Standards

⇒ Determine a theme of a story, drama, or poem from details in the text, including how characters in a story or drama respond to challenges or how the speaker in a poem reflects upon a topic; summarize the text.

⇒ Quote accurately from a text when explaining what the text says explicitly and when drawing inferences from the text.

⇒ Understand the impact of the Civil War on social issues.

Materials

⇒ *Bloody Shiloh* (page 111)

⇒ *"Bloody Shiloh" Response* (page 112)

⇒ *Shiloh: A Requiem* (page 114)

⇒ *"Shiloh: A Requiem" Response* (page 115)

⇒ *Let's Compare! The Battle of Shiloh* (page 116)

⇒ *Thinking About the Civil War!* (page 117)

⇒ pencils

⇒ highlighters

Comparing the Texts

After students complete the lessons for each text, have them work in pairs or groups to reread both texts and complete the *Let's Compare! The Battle of Shiloh* activity page (page 116). Finally, students can work to complete the *Thinking About the Civil War!* matrix (page 117). The matrix activities allow students to work on the important literacy skills of reading, writing, vocabulary, and fluency.

Answer Key

"Bloody Shiloh" Response (page 112)

1. A. at dawn, during breakfast

2. General Grant sees his men fleeing the fight and forces them to turn around and keep fighting. Then, the next morning, Grant orders his men to fight again.

3. Lincoln defends Grant's decision because he was tired of *other leaders who were backing down from big battles.*

"Shiloh: A Requiem" Response (page 115)

1. B. a church

2. *Swallows* appear at the beginning and end of the poem and convey silence as they are *still* and *hushed.*

3. The poet does not take sides. There is no proof or evidence that he is for the North or the South. Rather, the poet writes how the suffering brings the soldiers together so that by evening they are friends who are not concerned with fame or their country.

Let's Compare! The Battle of Shiloh (page 116)

Groups' scripts will vary. Check that the content in the scripts relates to both texts in the unit.

Nonfiction Text Teacher Notes
Bloody Shiloh

Lesson Steps	Teacher Think Alouds
Ready, Set, Predict! • Distribute the text to students and display a larger version. Read the title aloud. Ask students to do a quick and quiet text walk. • Ask partners to predict the author's purpose for writing this text using the following: *I think the author wrote this text to* _____ (e.g., *inform, persuade, entertain*) *because* _____.	
Go! • Have students read the text independently. Ask them to circle any numbers they see in the text. • Discuss which number was the largest they circled. What is that number referencing? What does it say about the Battle of Shiloh? • Read the text aloud as students follow along. Be sure to model fluent reading.	"The largest number I circled in the text is 23,000. That is how many Americans died during the battle. This detail helps show me that the Battle of Shiloh was one of the bloodiest and most tragic battles of the Civil War."
Reread to Clarify • Tell students to reread the text in small groups to clarify. Ask them to underline parts they found confusing and would like to clarify. • Ask groups to discuss their underlined parts using the following: *The part where* _____ *is confusing, so we* _____ (e.g., *reread, read on*).	
Reread to Question • Invite the groups to reread the text to question. Have each member create a question about General Sherman or General Grant. The other members can mark the answers to the questions with asterisks (*). • Have students respond to the question and prompts on page 112.	"By marking the answers to my group members' questions, I am able to better understand the text."
Reread to Summarize and Respond • Tell partners to reread text to summarize. Ask them to create written conversations between the two characters in the text. • Invite partners to perform their scripts for the class.	"Before we write our conversation, we decide which characters we will be. Then I'll write a line. My partner will write back to me and so on. By writing the conversation, my partner and I will better understand the text."

*Note: For more tips, engagement strategies, and fluency options to include in this lesson, see pages 122–128.

Name:_____ Date:_____

Bloody Shiloh

In 1862, the Confederate leaders created a plan to take control of Tennessee. They decided to attack the Union forces under General Ulysses S. Grant. The Northern soldiers were camping near Shiloh, Tennessee, and did not suspect anything.

At dawn on April 6, 1862, some Union men were eating their breakfasts when they heard a rebel yell. Union General William Sherman saw rebels streaming out from the woods. He rallied his men to stand firm. Sherman's men fought fiercely. Other Northern soldiers ran away from the fight.

General Grant raced to the battle from a few miles away. He found soldiers running away from the fight. He turned them around, and they fought the Southerners all day long. At nightfall, Confederate General Beauregard called off the battle and claimed a victory for the South.

The next morning, Grant ordered a counterattack. The Northerners attacked across the fields where bodies still lay from the day before. That afternoon Beauregard and the Confederates retreated. More than 23,000 Americans were dead.

The Northerners were angry with Grant for not being ready for the attack. They felt he should have prevented all the deaths. President Abraham Lincoln defended him by saying, "I can't spare this man. He fights." Lincoln was frustrated with his other leaders who were backing down from big battles.

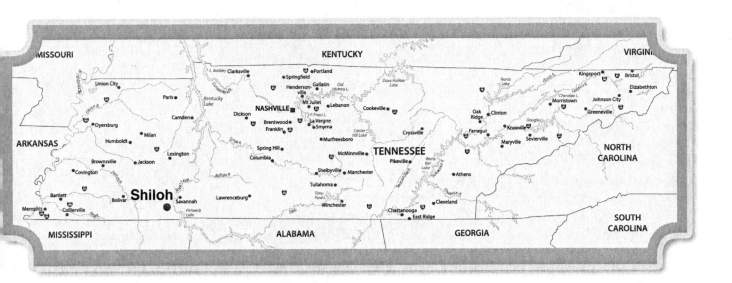

"Bloody Shiloh" Response

Directions: Reread the text on page 111 to answer each question.

1. What time of day did the rebels attack the Union soldiers at Shiloh?

   Ⓐ at dawn, during breakfast

   Ⓒ in the late afternoon

   Ⓑ at nightfall, while the Northern soldiers were sleeping

   Ⓓ in the late morning

2. When General Grant arrives on the scene, what does he do? How does he handle the situation?

   _____

   _____

   _____

   _____

   _____

3. Why did Lincoln defend Grant's decision? Use evidence from the text to support your answer.

   _____

   _____

   _____

   _____

   _____

Fiction Text Teacher Notes
Shiloh: A Requiem

		Lesson Steps	Teacher Think Alouds
	Ready, Set, Predict!	• Distribute the text to students and display a larger version. Read the title aloud. Ask students if they know what the word *requiem* means. Tell them that Shiloh is the name of a battle in the Civil War. • Ask students to write everything they know about the Civil War. If they do not have any prior knowledge of the war, they can predict what they think the text will be about.	"A requiem is a piece of music or composition in honor of the dead. Shiloh is the name of a battle that occurred during the Civil War. Knowing this helps me better understand what the poem is about."
	Go!	• Have students read the text independently and silently. Ask them to circle any words or phrases they find interesting. • Read the poem aloud to students. Model good fluency and tone. Discuss how reading fluently helps convey meaning.	"Are the words clearer in the poem when I read the poem, or when you read the poem? Does hearing me read the poem fluently help you better understand the poem, or is it easier to understand the poem when you read it yourself?"
	Reread to Clarify	• Tell students to reread the text to clarify. Ask them to highlight any words they find tricky. • Pair students. Have them switch their tricky words with their partners. Have them work to clarify each others' tricky words using the following: *The word/phrase _____ is tricky, so we _____* (e.g., *look it up, reread*).	"My partner circled the word *foemen*. I look it up in the dictionary, and it says 'an enemy of war.' We then talk about how the soldiers fought during the day but were friends at night when the fighting ceased."
	Reread to Question	• Place students in small groups. Ask them what the theme of the poem is. Have them discuss how they think the speaker in the poem feels about the battle and if this relates to the theme. • Ask groups to reread the poem to question. Have group members ask one another questions about how the author feels about the battle. • Have students respond to the question and prompts on page 115.	
	Reread to Summarize and Respond	• Tell students to reread the poem to summarize. Have them rewrite the poem in their own words. • Invite students to pair-share their new poems. • Review the close reading strategies with students by singing the song on page 128.	"When I reread the first part, I summarize it by saying 'The swallows are flying low on a dark day.'"

*Note: For more tips, engagement strategies, and fluency options to include in this lesson, see pages 122–128.

Social Studies Texts

Shiloh: A Requiem

by Herman Melville

Skimming lightly, wheeling still,
The swallows fly low
Over the field in clouded days,
The forest-field of Shiloh—
Over the field where April rain
Solaced the parched one stretched in pain
Through the pause of night
That followed the Sunday fight
Around the church of Shiloh—
The church so lone, the log-built one,
That echoed to many a parting groan
And natural prayer
Of dying foemen mingled there—
Foemen at morn, but friends at eve—
Fame or country least their care:
(What like a bullet can undeceive!)
But now they lie low,
While over them the swallows skim,
And all is hushed at Shiloh.

"Shiloh: A Requiem" Response

Directions: Reread the poem on page 114 to answer each question.

1. Around what structure does the battle take place?

   (A) a cannon   (C) a home

   (B) a church   (D) none of the above

2. What appears at the beginning and end of the poem? What tone does this convey?

   _____

   _____

   _____

   _____

   _____

   _____

3. Whose side is the poet on: the North's or South's? How do you know?

   _____

   _____

   _____

   _____

   _____

   _____

Social Studies Texts

Let's Compare!
The Battle of Shiloh

Directions: Reread both texts. Work in a small group to write a dialogue between a Northern and a Southern soldier based on the information you learned from both texts. Before you write your dialogue, fill out the form below. You may wish to include an introductory statement to set up the dialogue.

Character Name	Description

Setting

_____

_____

_____

Summary

_____

_____

_____

_____

_____

Now, complete the checklist below.

	Type or write your dialogue.
	Print out a copy for each student in your group.
	Read through your script as a group.
	Make any changes that are needed.
	Practice reading your script with your group for fluency.
	When you are ready, perform your script for your class!

Thinking About the Civil War!

Directions: Choose at least two of these activities to complete.

Radical Reading

There are five paragraphs in the "Bloody Shiloh" text. Reread each paragraph and write one or two words in the margin that summarize each paragraph.

Fun Fluency

Practice reciting "Shiloh: A Requiem" fluently. The tone of the poem is serious and somber; your voice should reflect this. When you are comfortable with the poem, recite it for a war veteran or member of the military or on a patriotic holiday.

Wonderful Words

War is a controversial topic. There are some people that believe war is never the answer. Others believe war is necessary to end some conflicts. Fold a sheet of paper in half. On one side of the sheet write the cons of war. On the other side of the sheet write the pros of war. At the bottom write a sentence stating your opinion on the matter.

Wacky Writing

Imagine you are a tour guide at Shiloh Battlefield Visitor Center in Shiloh, Tennessee. Use the information from the texts to write a script for your tour. Practice giving your tour of the battlefield. Then, take friends or family on your imaginary tour!

References Cited

Brassel, Danny, and Timothy Rasinski. 2008. *Comprehension that Works: Taking Students Beyond Ordinary Understanding to Deep Comprehension*. Huntington Beach, CA: Shell Education.

Common Core State Standards Initiative. 2010. *Common Core State Standards for English Language Arts & Literacy in History/Social Studies, Science, and Technical Subjects*. Washington, DC: National Governors Association Center for Best Practices and the Council of Chief State School Officers.

Fisher, David, and Nancy Frey. 2012. "Close Reading in Elementary Schools." *The Reading Teacher* 66 (3): 179–188.

Hattie, John A. 2008. *Visible Learning: A Synthesis of Over 800 Meta-Analyses Relating to Achievement*. Oxford, UK: Routledge.

Oczkus, Lori D. 2010. *Reciprocal Teaching at Work: Powerful Strategies and Lessons for Improving Reading Comprehension 2nd Edition*. Newark, DE: International Reading Association.

Oczkus, Lori D. 2012. *Just the Facts: Close Reading and Comprehension of Informational Text*. Huntington Beach, CA: Shell Education and International Reading Association (copublication).

Palincsar, Annemarie Sullivan, and Ann L. Brown. 1986. "Interactive Teaching to Promote Independent Learning from Text." *The Reading Teacher* 39 (8): 771–777.

Rasinski, Timothy V. 2010. *The Fluent Reader: Oral and Silent Reading Strategies for Building Fluency, Word Recognition and Comprehension 2nd Edition*. New York: Scholastic.

Rasinski, Timothy V. and Lorraine Griffith. 2010. *Building Fluency Through Practice and Performance*. Huntington Beach, CA: Shell Education.

Rosenshine, Barak, and Carla Meister. 1994. "Reciprocal Teaching: A Review of the Research." *Review of Educational Research* 64 (4): 479–530.

Correlation to the Standards

Shell Education is committed to producing educational materials that are research and standards based. In this effort, we have correlated all of our products to the academic standards of all 50 states, the District of Columbia, the Department of Defense Dependents Schools, and all Canadian provinces.

How to Find Standards Correlations

To print a customized correlation report of this product for your state, visit our website at http://www.shelleducation.com and follow the on-screen directions. If you require assistance in printing correlation reports, please contact our Customer Service Department at 1-877-777-3450.

Purpose and Intent of Standards

Legislation mandates that all states adopt academic standards that identify the skills students will learn in kindergarten through grade twelve. Many states also have standards for Pre-K. This same legislation sets requirements to ensure the standards are detailed and comprehensive.

Standards are designed to focus instruction and guide adoption of curricula. Standards are statements that describe the criteria necessary for students to meet specific academic goals. They define the knowledge, skills, and content students should acquire at each level. Standards are also used to develop standardized tests to evaluate students' academic progress. Teachers are required to demonstrate how their lessons meet state standards. State standards are used in the development of all of our products, so educators can be assured they meet the academic requirements of each state.

Common Core State Standards

The activities in this book are aligned to the Common Core State Standards (CCSS). The chart on pages 120–121 lists the standards addressed in each lesson. Specific standards are also listed on the first page of each lesson.

McREL Compendium

We use the Mid-Continent Research for Education and Learning (McREL) Compendium to create standards correlations. Each year, McREL analyzes state standards and revises the compendium. By following this procedure, McREL is able to produce a general compilation of national standards. Each lesson in this product is based on one or more McREL standards. The chart on page 121 lists the standards addressed in each lesson.

TESOL and WIDA Standards

The activities in this book promote English language development for English language learners. The chart on page 121 lists the standards addressed in each lesson.

Correlation to the Standards (cont)

College and Career Readiness Standards	Lessons
Literacy.RL.5.1—Quote accurately from a text when explaining what the text says explicitly and when drawing inferences from the text.	Extreme Weather (p. 19); Triangles (p. 46); The Metric System (p. 55)
Literacy.RL.5.2—Determine a theme of a story, drama, or poem from details in the text, including how characters in a story or drama respond to challenges or how the speaker in a poem reflects upon a topic; summarize the text.	Prejudice (p. 10); Abraham Lincoln (p. 28); Adding Fractions (p. 37); The Civil War (p. 109)
Literacy.RL.5.3—Compare and contrast two or more characters, settings, or events in a story or drama, drawing on specific details in the text (e.g., how characters interact).	Atoms (p. 73); Lewis and Clark (p. 100)
Literacy.RL.5.4—Determine the meaning of words and phrases as they are used in a text, including figurative language such as metaphors and similes.	Stars (p. 64)
Literacy.RL.5.5—Explain how a series of chapters, scenes, or stanzas fits together to provide the overall structure of a particular story, drama, or poem.	American Indians and Westward Expansion (p. 91)
Literacy.RL.5.6—Describe how a narrator's or speaker's point of view influences how events are described.	Cells (p. 82)
Literacy.RI.5.1—Quote accurately from a text when explaining what the text says explicitly and when drawing inferences from the text.	The Metric System (p. 55); American Indians and Westward Expansion (p. 91); The Civil War (p. 109)
Literacy.RI.5.2—Determine two or more main ideas of a text and explain how they are supported by key details; summarize the text.	Stars (p. 64)
Literacy.RI.5.3—Explain the relationships or interactions between two or more individuals, events, ideas, or concepts in a historical, scientific, or technical text based on specific information in the text.	Prejudice (p. 10); Extreme Weather (p. 19); Lewis and Clark (p. 100)
Literacy.RI.5.4—Determine the meaning of general academic and domain-specific words and phrases in a text relevant to a *grade 5 topic or subject area*.	Adding Fractions (p. 37); Triangles (p. 46); Atoms (p. 73)
Literacy.RI.5.7—Draw on information from multiple print or digital sources, demonstrating the ability to locate an answer to a question quickly or to solve a problem efficiently.	Cells (p. 82)
Literacy.RI.5.8—Explain how an author uses reasons and evidence to support particular points in a text, identifying which reasons and evidence support which point(s).	Abraham Lincoln (p. 28)
Literacy.SL.5.1—Engage effectively in a range of collaborative discussions with diverse partners on *grade 5 topics and texts*, building on others' ideas and expressing their own clearly.	Extreme Weather (p. 19)
Literacy.L.5.5—Demonstrate understanding of figurative language, word relationships, and nuances in word meanings.	Prejudice (p. 10); Abraham Lincoln (p. 28)
Math.Content5.NF.A2—Solve word problems involving addition and subtraction of fractions referring to the same whole, including cases of unlike denominators, e.g., by using visual fraction models or equations to represent the problem. Use benchmark fractions and number sense of fractions to estimate mentally and assess the reasonableness of answers.	Adding Fractions (p. 37)

Correlation to the Standards *(cont)*

College and Career Readiness Standards	Lessons
Math.Content.5.G.B.3—Understand that attributes belonging to a category of two-dimensional figures also belong to all subcategories of that category.	Triangles (p. 46)
Math.Content.5.MD.A.1—Convert among different-sized standard measurement units within a given measurement system (e.g., convert 5 cm to 0.05 m), and use these conversions in solving multi-step, real world problems.	The Metric System (p. 55)

McREL Standards	Lessons
Science 3.2—Knows that matter is made up of tiny particles called atoms, and different arrangements of atoms into groups compose all substances.	Atoms (p. 73)
Science 3.5—Knows that astronomical objects in space are massive in size and are separated from one another by vast distances.	Stars (p. 64)
Science 5.2—Knows that cells convert energy obtained from food to carry on the many functions needed to sustain life.	Cells (p. 82)
United States History 19.1—Understands significant events for Native American tribes in the late 19th century and how they responded.	American Indians and Westward Expansion (p. 91)
Civics 9.2—Knows about expeditions of American explorers.	Lewis and Clark (p. 100)
Civics 14.3—Understands the impact of the Civil War on social issues.	The Civil War (p. 109)
Math 3.2—Adds and subtracts fractions with unlike denominators.	Adding Fractions (p. 37)
Math 4.4—Solves problems involving units of measurement and converts answers to a larger or smaller unit within the same system (i.e., standard or metric).	The Metric System (p. 55)
Math 5.3—Understands the defining properties of triangles.	Triangles (p. 46)

TESOL/WIDA Standards	Lessons
English language learners **communicate** for **social, intercultural**, and **instructional** purposes within the school setting	All Lessons
English language learners **communicate** information, ideas, and concepts necessary for academic success in the area of **language arts**	All Lessons
English language learners **communicate** information, ideas, and concepts necessary for academic success in the area of **mathematics**	All Mathematics Lessons
English language learners **communicate** information, ideas, and concepts necessary for academic success in the area of **science**	All Science Lessons
English language learners **communicate** information, ideas, and concepts necessary for academic success in the area of **social studies**	All Social Studies Lessons

Tips for Implementing the Lessons

Lesson Tips

Below are additional tips and suggestions you may wish to do with students as you implement the lessons.

- Choose 4 to 6 words from each text pair and place them on a word wall for students to observe. Students can complete various word activities with the words.

- Use online resources, such as video clips or audio clips, to help students better understand the content.

- Have students research the authors of some of the texts or research more about the content in the texts so students can gain more knowledge.

- Keep a running list of strategies students use to clarify words, phrases, and ideas. Have the list visible for students to use as they clarify texts (e.g., reread, read on, sound out).

- Choose a long word from a text and present the letters of the word to students in alphabetical order, dividing the letters into consonants and vowels. Guide students to make a series of 5 to 10 words with the letters by giving them word meanings or clues to guess the words.

- Play WORDO with students by having them draw 4 x 4 matrixes. Display 16 to 20 words from the texts. Have students write one word in each box. Randomly select a word and call out its definition. Have each student mark the box the word is in. The first student to get four words in a straight or diagonal line calls out, "Wordo!"

- Invite students to act out words, sentences, or main ideas of a text with or without using their voices. Have the rest of the class guess what is being acted out.

Pacing Tips

Below are suggested options for implementing the lessons with students.

An Ideal Pacing Plan	If Working with Longer Texts
Day 1: Nonfiction text close reading lesson/follow-up activities	**Day 1:** Complete the close reading steps, including predicting, clarifying, questioning, and summarizing, for the first portion of the text.
Day 2: Fiction text close reading lesson/ follow-up activities	
Day 3: Compare the texts/follow-up activities	**Day 2:** Running through all four steps again for the second portion of the text.
Day 4: Reread texts/follow-up activities	**Note:** The follow-up activities should be done at the conclusion of the entire reading of a text.
Day 5: Reread texts/share follow-up activities	

Strategies

Engagement Strategies

Make learning memorable by using the following engagement strategies.

Discussion in Pairs	Throughout the lessons, have students talk with partners or groups to enhance comprehension. Conduct whole-group sharing after partners discuss their responses.	

Mark or Code with Text Symbols	Have students work independently or in groups to mark the text using symbols to show their thinking. Provide copies of the text for students and display a copy of the text for the class to view as you demonstrate. Symbols may include: + main idea √ details # cool idea ☺ favorite part Have students use different colored pencils, highlighters, or markers as they read. They can circle, underline, or box portions of the text.

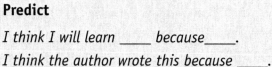

Discussion Sentence Frames

Have students use discussion sentence frames when sharing responses with others. Frames help keep students on task during discussions. Some examples include:

Predict *I think I will learn _____ because_____.* *I think the author wrote this because _____.*	**Clarify** *I didn't get the word/sentence _____, so I _____.*
Question *Who, what, when, where, why, how, I wonder _____.*	**Summarize** *This is about _____.* *The main idea is _____.*

Close Reading Props

Bring in a pair of goofy glasses or a magnifying glass to hold up when it is time to read a text closely. You may wish to duplicate the glasses or magnifying glass patterns found on page 126 for students to use during the lessons.

Glasses Tell students, "Close reading is like putting on special glasses as you reread the text to figure it out."	**Magnifying Glass** Tell students, "Close reading is like using a magnifying glass to help you understand the text as you reread it."

Sing to the Strategies

Help students remember the different purposes for rereading by creating a song with verses for each of the reciprocal teaching strategies. A song option can be found on page 128.

Strategies *(cont)*

Gestures or Props for Each Strategy

Use gestures or props to help students remember the close reading strategies as they closely read a text.

Predict: Use a physical crystal ball or pretend to rub a crystal ball to predict what will happen or what the text is about using clues from the text.	**Question:** Use a physical microphone or use a fist to make a microphone to interview one another asking and answering questions.
Clarify: Use glasses or a magnifying glass. You can also use your arms: parallel to show a "pause" button, to point to the left for rewind, and to the right for reading on to help clarify tricky words in a text.	**Summarize:** Use a lasso (with yarn or string) or pretend to wield a lasso to rope in the "main ideas and details" of a text.

Adapted from Lori Oczkus (2010)

Fluency Strategies

The chart below lists various fluency techniques to use with students.

Model Fluent Reading	Teacher or other proficient reader reads the text to students. After the reading, teacher leads students in a discussion of the content of the text *and* the way in which the teacher or reader reads the text (e.g., expression, phrasing, pacing).
Assisted Reading— Choral Reading	Groups of students read the text orally together. Students who are more fluent readers provide an assist to students who are less fluent.
Assisted Reading— Paired Reading	Two readers read a text orally together. One reader is more proficient than the other. The more proficient reader acts as a model for the less fluent one.
Assisted Reading— Audio-recorded Reading	A student reads a text while at the same time listening to a fluent recording of the same text. The recorded reading acts as a model for the student.
Assisted Reading— Echo Reading	Teacher reads the text aloud while tracking the print for students to see. After the text has been read aloud, children imitate, or echo, the teacher as they visually track the text.
Repeated Reading	Students read a text several times orally and silently for different purposes. One purpose for all rereading is to improve students' fluency (e.g., word recognition, automaticity, and expression).
Phrased Text Reading	The teacher or student marks the appropriate phrase boundaries in a text with slash marks. The student then reads the text, pausing at the marked locations. Readers who lack fluency often read in a word-by-word manner that limits the meaning of the passage. These visual cues give students support in reading in meaningful phrases.

Adapted from Timothy Rasinski (2010)

Assessment Options

Aside from students' work on the activity pages, there are many opportunities to assess students during each step of the close reading process. Use the chart below to guide your assessments.

Ready, Set, Predict!

Does the student . . .

- skim the text/visuals to make logical predictions?
- relate relevant prior knowledge?
- anticipate author's purpose?
- predict topic/theme?
- anticipate how the text is organized?

Go!

Does the student . . .

- make an attempt to read the text independently?
- follow along during the teacher read-aloud?
- mark unfamiliar words and ideas?
- participate in shared readings; follow along?
- identify what makes the teacher's reading fluent?

Reread to Clarify

Does the student . . .

- reread to mark words they want to know or clarify?
- identify words/lines that help students visualize?
- identify more than one "fix it" strategy such as sounding out, chopping words into parts, rereading, reading on?

Reread to Question

Does the student . . .

- reread to ask or create questions for peers?
- reread to answer text-dependent questions using text evidence?
- confidently ask and answer questions?

Reread to Summarize and Respond

Does the student . . .

- select main ideas and details to summarize?
- summarize selection in order?
- use key vocabulary to summarize?
- mark text to show responses using symbols?

  + main idea   √ details   # cool idea   ☺ favorite part

- compare/contrast the fiction and nonfiction texts?

Templates

Glasses

Directions: Decorate the glasses. Then, cut them out and glue them on a craft stick. Use them as you closely read text.

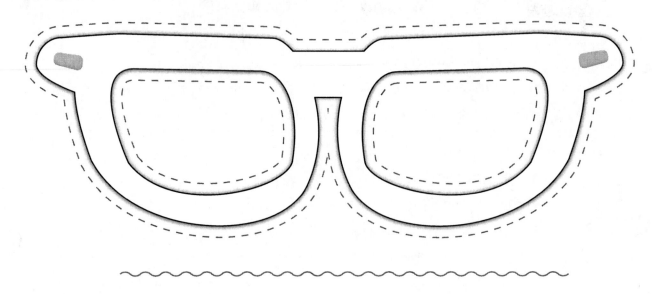

Magnifying Glass

Directions: Decorate the magnifying glass. Then, cut it out and use it as you closely read text.

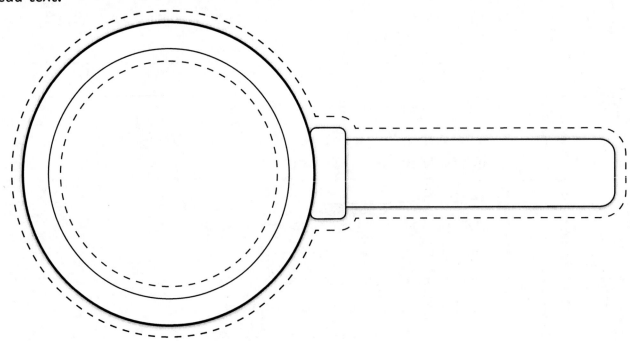